Praise for M

An emotional journey into a fascinating world of family, work and travel. The book leaves you with a desire for more.

Lisa Allison

I have read your courageous account of life in African towns, your professional and personal dilemmas, and been both disturbed and admiring.

Dr Aurora Couto, author

Got your book and read it without stopping ... very very interesting ... life in Africa... At times very sad...

Rita Mathias

A fascinating insight into an extraordinary life, rich in cultural detail and emotion. A very moving account.

June Parker

Mama Mganga Woman Doctor

Mimi Correia-Afonso Desai

Desert Rose Publishing
Bristol and London

Desert Rose Publishing
Bristol and London

All the events in this book are true. Some names have been changed in the interest of privacy. Any similarity of these names to the names of any living person is purely coincidental. The narratives herein are faithful to my own experience though others may remember things differently. My motives have always remained clean and I intend no harm.

First published in 2014
Republished with revisions 2015

ISBN: 978-0-9931252-4-9
Mama Mganga Woman Doctor

Dedication

This book is dedicated to my children and grandchildren from whom I have learnt more about Life and living than I have ever taught them.

"Patients will love you and patients will hate you, but don't let the Love go to your head, or the Hate to your heart." A rather senior doctor dropped these words of caution into my very junior ears, a long time ago. This book is about that Love, that Hate, and about my patients, about those who loved, those who hated, and those who were indifferent but who, in one way or another, for better or for worse, affected my life. It is also about my struggle to integrate into my husband's community, so alien to me. In this I truly failed... But, in retrospect, I think I did not really want to succeed.

About the Author

Mimi Correia-Afonso Desai was born in 1932 in Goa, at that time Portuguese India where she spent her childhood and teenage years. She qualified as a doctor from Bombay University and worked in India, Tanzania, and then England, where she now lives.

Her interests are geology, travel, languages, ancient history and knitting. She has three children and six grandchildren. This is her first book.

Acknowledgements

I am deeply grateful to:

my daughter Reethah for her belief in me, her unfailing encouragement and practical and emotional support, and the countless hours she put in – I truly could not have written this book without her;

my grandson Anton-Jari for his enthusiasm and all his countless hours of hard work in editing, formatting and proof-reading, and without which my writings would not have been transformed into the book you are reading now;

and Klaus Traber for reading my manuscript and making positive and constructive comments and suggestions.

Contents

Preface

I'm sitting comfortably on the cosy, cane rocking chair my three children gave me on my 50th birthday. Before me lies The Chest. I tremble because I have kept The Chest locked and the contents out of sight and out of mind for decades. Half a century on and some 3000 miles from the scene, I sit with an ache in my heart, my hand trembling over the key I hold, the key to The Treasure Chest of memories of my life and years in Africa. The key is not golden but made of sturdy iron, rusty in places and The Chest is not made of fancy or exotic wood. It is not carved; it is down-to-earth pine wood, well weathered and tired-looking – much like myself, I expect. The hinges and lock are rusty and dull. I have had the key for a very long time. It was never lost, in fact, but... But with trembling hands I pick up the key...

"Mimi, you are a girl with great courage" had said a cousin once when I was young and at a time when I most needed to hear it. If that is still so, go on, woman, turn the key and peer inside. What are you waiting for? Will The Chest be a Pandora's Box and only let out trouble? Or... Go on, woman, you won't find out if you don't open it, will you?

Mimi as a medical student (1955 - left)
Mimi when she met Ashok on a student trip
to South India (1956 - right)

Arrival

Africa! Here I come at last! Mombasa! How romantic! I am excited. I am anxious. I am terrified. But I wouldn't have it any different. AFRICA! A dream come true! The Dark Continent I have heard it called. Dark? The brightness of the sun is blinding. It's hard to see even a few yards away.

Yet my mind was seeing into the distance of time. What could I see? Excitement, happiness, sadness, despair, turmoil – so many things I could see whirling and whizzing past my mind's eye. It was like looking into a crystal ball. But what the gypsy sees in a crystal ball is all make-believe: words to please your ears, to make your predictions and your price worthwhile. This, on the other hand, was very real indeed. In retrospect, Africa gave me all those things and more, and in very large doses. Africa is large and all Africa experience is large to match. I have never been drunk on alcohol, but I have been inebriated with happiness, excitement, sadness and despair and coconut milk. Did I see or taste promise that moment when I stepped into Africa? A promise of what? I can't honestly say I did. The anxiety of the situation overwhelmed all other thoughts and feelings.

From head in the clouds I was brought firmly and sharply to feet on the ground. There was baby Malini, parched with the heat and clamouring for a feed. There was all the noise and bustle of an African port: the deafening sounds, the overwhelming smells, the sight of a sea of dark bodies I had never seen before, the overpowering heat. "Pull yourself together," I heard myself say above all the tumult. "You need all your wits about you!" I had never witnessed such frenetic activity. Indian families on the dock waving excitedly as they spot the new arrivals on the ship. Cranes, trucks, various vehicles, hustle and bustle. I had never seen an African before and there I was with hundreds everywhere I looked. Africans and Indians. Not a European in sight. I expect they all flew. Most of them didn't have to dig deep into their pockets to travel to Africa. Their governments paid for travel and a life of luxury.

Everyone on the ship seems to have someone on the dock and is waving frantically… everyone but me. Baby M and I have no welcome from this Continent I so long to discover… and which I will come to love so much later. Presently, out of the swarm of humans, two seem to take possession of all my belongings and are pulling, pushing and rolling all my luggage out of the cabin, down the gangway and into the landing area. I panic but Rama, my cabin mate who also travelled with a young baby from Bombay, is soon by my side and puts a reassuring hand on my shoulder. “Don’t worry”, she says, “they know what they are doing. Nothing will be lost.” I look anxiously around into the crowd of Indians who have come to receive their relatives. Rama spots her husband and her brother who are frantically waving. I look and peer in the bright light and see no familiar face at all.

Rama comes to meet me with her husband. Her family live in Mombasa. “Would you like to come home with us?” She is kind and concerned for me. “I can’t, I must wait for my parents-in-law.” I am very tempted to accept her invitation but have to decline. My parents-in-law, originating from Gujarat, north-west India, are expected to come to meet me at the dock and take me to their home in Tanga, 120 miles away, but I see nobody looking for me. Where on earth are they? I wonder and worry.

Eventually my luggage consisting of 10 packages – trunks, suitcases, holdalls and baby’s wicker bassinette – is down neatly on the ground and piled up somewhere on the dock. I handle East African shillings for the first time and pay the coolie in my first dealing with a black man. He is pleasant and friendly and muscular with all the lifting and carrying of luggage he has to do.

I can’t wait much longer in this heat with no drink, no way to move away to the shade leaving the luggage, and nothing to do but sit and wait. I sit on top of a trunk with my earthly belongings about me, the smallest yet most precious of all, my first-born baby girl Malini. She is hot and thirsty. I am glad she is breastfed – at least I don't have to worry about preparing a bottle. I breastfeed her right there on the dock, sitting on a trunk, with hundreds of African coolies all around! But I am dressed in a sari and a sari has umpteen uses, one of which is to hide a baby under the *pallow* so it can be breastfed in total privacy.

Bombay was hot at most times and hotter at others but we had not been prepared for those extreme temperatures, the likes of which were not part of my dream. The experience of arrival in Africa was like jumping into the deep end of a dark, boiling whirlpool.

Anxiety overshadows my excitement and sweat dampens more than my sari blouse. I sit on the trunk with baby in my arms for what seems an eternity. I am tired, hot, hungry, thirsty and feeling very sorry for myself. Such a disappointment, an anticlimax after all I have imagined and dreamt Africa would be. I had dreamt of jungles and snakes, large rivers teeming with crocodiles and the sound of not too distant drums, but this is a little lick at Inferno. The heat is sweltering but my palms feel cold and clammy. And I am not so sure that what I feel going down my spine is a trickle of sweat.

"*Mama, nakwenda vapi*?" Asks a porter. What am I to answer? I don't understand a word of Kiswahili. I suddenly see my parents-in-law, Ba and Bapuji, coming towards me. I immediately pull my *pallow* over the head. When they reach me I bend down and touch Bapuji's feet to show my respect as is the custom in my husband's culture. He lightly touches me on the head and says something I don't understand. I suppose it is a blessing. Then he touches my baby on the head and says the same thing. I then get up and go to Ba and bend down again to touch her feet. After blessing me and the baby by placing her hand on our heads, she gently pulls me up and takes the baby. They both look at baby M and remark how much she looks like her father as a baby. The coolie loads my luggage onto a pick-up borrowed from a *Bohora* (member of a certain sect of Muslims) friend and which came with a driver. Ba, who has come prepared with food and drink, takes out a flask and pours me some coffee which I drink thirstily.

In Africa you never know the duration of a journey. You go prepared for all eventualities. I don't remember a single long journey when we didn't have at least one puncture. They had had two on the way to pick me up, hence the delay. A lot of the roads were dirt tracks with sharp pebbles and drivers were so rash. In the next few years I saw many fatal accidents, some with gruesome results.

We are soon speeding along the 120 miles towards Tanga, our home-to-be for the next few years. On the way home I was quiet. I wasn't supposed to talk in front of my father-in-law. Ba and Bapuji talked between themselves but my Gujarati was not good enough to understand all they said. On the journey from Mombasa to Tanga we had one inevitable puncture, but finally arrived at our destination after some three hours.

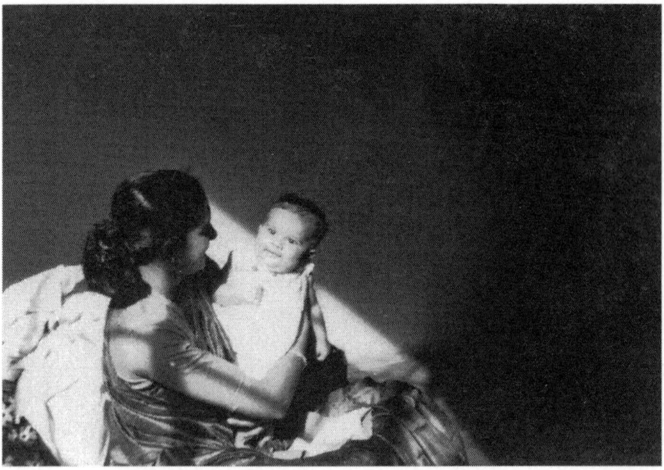

Mimi with baby Malini (1959)

Hallo Tanga

Good morning to a new country in a new continent. To a new culture, a new language… wait, no. Two! Gujarati and Kiswahili. As a new mother it wasn't going to be easy, to say the least. It was frightening. It was challenging. It was exciting. Would I be able to cope with it? Nothing to do but face it all and see what happens.

Bapuji owned the house where he and Ba lived and brought up 10 children. He also owned the house across the little street which he rented out but the outhouse at the back was vacant and that was mainly my home for the next week. It was oppressively hot and there was no fan to alleviate the discomfort. My poor baby screamed all night and my milk was rapidly drying. The next morning Ba complained. "The whole town could hear the baby's cries!" Was that a statement or an accusation? She did not ask if anything was wrong. What neighbours said mattered enormously, more than my happiness or the baby's welfare.

Baby and I slept in the outhouse at night but spent the day at Bapuji's house. In the front room there was a double bed, two armchairs and a coffee table.

Bapuji spent most of his time in his bedroom which was fine by me as I was not to stay in his presence. When he sat in the front room, if I needed to go in or out of the house, I had to cover my head and never speak to him. One day Ba said I didn't cover my head well enough and the *pallow* should go right low over my forehead. When not able to use the front room, the only other place I could be in was the kitchen. I knew nothing of Gujarati cooking and Ba with great patience taught me to roll *rotlis* (Gujarati chapattis), and cook vegetables and dals. She would put spices in my hand and make me throw them into the pot.

In that week I learnt a great deal not only about Gujarati cooking but about Gujarati culture and traditions and got to know my mother-in-law. She was not an attractive woman but she was amazingly good to me, especially considering I came from a totally different culture. By the tenets of her culture she should have treated me like dirt, but she had lots of patience with me and I found I felt comfortable in her presence. It struck me how very different my culture was from my husband's, especially in the treatment of a daughter-in-law.

In my family a daughter-in-law was treated like a Princess. We had several servants who did all the work and the daughter-in-law was referred to as *Okolbai* (The Bride) for the rest of her life. When she eventually had her own daughter-in-law she became

"Big Bride" and the new one "Little Bride". In contrast, in Ashok's culture a daughter-in-law was the lowest of the low. She was given neither love nor respect and treated as a second-class citizen. If a family was poor and there was not enough food to go round it was the daughter-in-law who went without.

Ashok had told me something more shocking about their community. A girl was given a dowry when she got married. Exactly how much depended on the inequality of the two parties. If a girl was ugly, dark-skinned, had no education, and a disability like a limp or squint, her market value was low and her father had to pay a bigger dowry. If, however, she was pretty, fair-skinned, well educated (and especially if she was more educated than the boy), her value was high and less dowry was paid. A sought-after girl of a 'higher' family could marry a humpback, drunkard, ignoramus or 'no-gooder' for next to nothing.

What about the boy? His marketable price was on the same terms, in reverse. It didn't matter if he was a half-wit, cock-eyed, drunk or hump-backed or worse. Once they were married and the dowry paid, the haggling didn't end there. Anything she needed for her personal use she still had to get from her own father. When she had her babies, she was told to get from her father absolutely everything that was needed right up to soap to wash the baby's clothes. Imagine my relief to discover that my new family was different! Although their standard of living was low, they earned my respect for their principles and for daring to be different from the rest of the inhabitants of Tanga, the likes of whom never earned my respect at all in all the years I spent there.

At the time only the youngest four of my husband's siblings were at home. Ashok being the second eldest, the siblings at home were very much younger than me. The youngest, Kishore and Shobha, were almost young enough to be my own children. Kishore was eight, young enough to drop his trousers in my presence without embarrassment, whilst Shoba still played with dolls. I made clothes for her and even for her dolls and I'm pleased she still remembers this… But in Gujarati culture a woman must give great respect to her husband's siblings, whatever their age. I had to address them by their name followed by *bhai* for boys and *ben* for girls. They in turn addressed me as *bhabhi*, a title for brother's wife. Despite everything I loved this title; it sounds so sweet.

Mimi in Raskazone Park (1960)

Rural Tanzania (1960)

Shobha on steps of Bapuji's house, India Street (1967)

Reethah, Jayesh, Malini in front of Bapuji's house (1967)

Monkey in the Zoo

It started the very first evening after my arrival and was to go on evening after evening. The town heard of "The Daughter-in-Law's Arrival" and people descended on the house en masse. They got together in groups, in gangs, sometimes droves, like vultures about to descend on a fresh kill. Anything up to 20 at once descended on us, the women of Tanga with children in tow but never their husbands. In Gujarati the word for "visit" is "to sit". And they literally came "to sit". You could hear their cackles and gaggles as they advanced. They swarmed in like a cloud of locusts all at the same time. After the invasion was over and they'd left I felt like a delicate blade of grass.

"*Kem cho, kem cho*" (how are you) it went on till they had all said it. "*Besso*" (please sit down) said Ba, and they all squatted on the floor in the front room. Ba came to fetch me and led me out to the front room to sit on the bed in the corner with baby. From the floor some 20 pairs of eyes looked up and stared. They didn't speak to me, though even if they had done I couldn't have understood very much anyway. I could see and hear them whispering to one another and was acutely aware that I was the subject of those whispers. From their faces and expressions it was clear that what they said was not complimentary.

I studied their faces and tried to read their thoughts. "Isn't she thin!"; "she's okay, I suppose"; "what sort of daughter-in-law would you expect in this house!"; "she doesn't have much jewellery on; can't come from a good family"; "baby has no *cajal*," (black used around a baby's eyes to prevent evil eye) "she doesn't know how to look after a baby"; "she calls herself a doctor. Doctor? She is a woman, how can she be a doctor? She must be a Nurse."; "I wonder if she will squat and eat on the floor with the in-laws?"

Do I sound paranoid? Well, whatever I saw in those eyes staring at me, it was not friendliness. I saw resentment, criticism, dislike. After all I was an outsider and shouldn't be there at all. And I was educated, a qualified doctor, whilst their girls had barely made it through school. But worst of all, they sat and stared. Stared at me. A myriad critical eyes.

The moment that the horde settled down Ba went into the kitchen, lit the Primus stove and made Gujarati *chai* (tea). It was fascinating to see Gujarati women make tea. Whether it was for five people or for 20, they placed a large saucepan on the stove on the floor, then, without bending, poured water into the pot, then milk and sugar – plenty of it. When it came to the boil they poured tea leaves from a can and when the colour was just right, tea *masala* (spices) was added, the Primus stove switched off, and the pot covered for a few minutes to infuse. The result was a delicious *masala chai.* It smelt wonderful and always tasted delicious and most refreshing. What amazed me was that they never measured anything, just drizzled, poured, dribbled and the result was not only perfect in taste, but the quantity was just right whatever the size of the horde. Over the years I came to love this *masala chai*, as did my children and grandchildren who still do today.

When they had drunk noisily from their saucers, they stared some more and then one by one they got up and one by one said "*owjoh*" (equivalent to "goodbye") and waddled out of the house to resume their cackling and gaggling and swoop on their next victim. It would be different at the next port of call or the one before; no one to stare at, nothing new to break the routine boredom and dullness of their lives. They would all cackle loudly and in sync as they murdered a few reputations. The house was suddenly quiet and I wished I was elsewhere; anywhere, as long as it was else.

Kundan, my 11 year old brother-in-law, came in with his usual smile and eyes shining with mischief. I do believe my four young in-laws saved my sanity. Kundan sat cross-legged on a chair opposite, hugging his knees with his hands and rocking. "Bhabhi, are you some kind of exotic animal?" His eyes were twinkling. "Why?", I asked. I felt like one. "Why do they all come and gape at you as if you are one? Like we do to the animals in the Zoo." With his youth in the absence of canniness, he had hit the nail precisely on the head. That was exactly how I felt but I couldn't tell him so; my Gujarati was not fluent enough. Kundan was a great joker and a joy to have around and in the years to come was to become my favourite brother-in-law and my children's favourite uncle.

* * *

Ba took me to visit friends. I remember particularly an old man, Pragjibhai, whom Ba and I went to visit. He was broad-minded, educated, intelligent and wise. While Ba talked to his wife, he came over and sat next to me and talked to me in English. It was such a treat, so refreshing. We had such an interesting and stimulating discussion that I forgot I was a *vahu* (daughter-in-law) and just behaved my normal self, talking to him like an equal as I was used to. On the way home Ba showed her displeasure. "You shouldn't talk to men like that, as if they are your equals, you must show respect".

That was just one of the many bombshells I was to receive. Out of all the people I had met so far, old Pragjibhai was the only person for whom I had felt respect. I soon discovered that the word "respect" was defined differently in our respective dictionaries. I wondered if I had gone down in the old man's esteem and lost his respect (by my definition), for having talked to him – a man old enough to be my grandfather – as an equal. In the short time that we met I felt a close attachment to the old man. I felt he understood me and empathised. I in turn could feel his life and his struggles, the result of him being different, above the humdrum of his community. He didn't fit in and neither did I. His past (as I imagined it) was an inspiration for my future. I had found in him a kindred spirit.

It soon transpired that Gujaratis did not give presents; they always gave money. How much? Well, that depended on the relationship to the other party and what they had given you in the past. I was appalled that everything was measured in terms of shillings. The custom was not to give a round figure. It was never 5, 10, 20, 50 or 100, but instead 6, 11, 21, 51 or 101. I never found out the reason. Was it to do with luck? People gave money to my baby, mostly six or eleven shillings. I carefully collected it all in a box for baby M for safe keeping until I decided what I should do with it or where to save it. I wasn't sure how I should save it for her, but for the moment it was safe. After a few days Ba asked for the money. I said "It is baby's money". "No it's not" she retorted.

"People gave baby money because in the past we gave money to their children or grandchildren. They are repaying *us*. It is *our* money." This money business. I still have not come to terms with that attitude.

In Laws

Ba and Bapuji were different. Unimaginably different from men and women in my culture, but even very different from men and women in their own. Having matriculated (taken exams, aged 16), Bapuji had left Gujarat at 16 to take up employment in Uganda. At 20 he had gone back to Gujarat to get himself a wife. Bapuji was tall, light-skinned and nice-looking. He must have been quite handsome in his youth. In contrast, Ba was short, dark-skinned and quite unattractive. She had had only a couple of years of schooling. I expect her parents must have given a large dowry as incentive as is the custom. As I learnt, in their community marriages were not only all arranged by the older generation and dowry given and taken, but the amount depended on several factors, like the sale of cattle.

One factor that didn't seem to come into it at all was what the bride's father could afford, let alone the question of love. I don't believe any girl ever married for nothing at all because any husband, however undesirable, was better than no husband at all. I thought it all very primitive. In my own community marriages were still arranged but the girl had a lot of say in the matter and, although dowry was still given, it didn't depend on the looks or education of the two parties, but rather the suitability of the couple. It was a lot more civilised. For me, of course, all dowry and arranged marriage was abhorrent, and this represented one of the primary reasons I was in my present predicament.

Ba and Bapuji seemed to have got on alright, Ba having had some 16 pregnancies of which four boys and six girls survived. Bapuji wanted each one, boys and girls, to have an education. As education was not free and Bapuji was only a clerk, the couple had to make a lot of sacrifices and I take my hat off to my in-laws for defying convention and focusing on what they considered their priorities. Incredibly, Bapuji managed to educate nine out of his 10 children – of the boys, two became doctors and two engineers, and of the six girls, two became teachers, two secretaries, and one, a pharmacist. Only the eldest daughter did not study beyond school as she was brought up by her grandparents in India for some reason.

They could not afford both school fees and servants so kept no 'houseboy' like every other family, a choice which had led to a loss of respect from the rest of the town. A houseboy was a male African servant who did all the hard work in a household: cleaning the house, washing and ironing clothes, carrying the shopping, washing dishes and scrubbing pans. The latter was done with coconut husk and wood ash from the cooking. This made the utensils gleam but was very harsh on the hands.

In their house all the work was done by the girls, including the scrubbing of pans with coconut husk and ash. The girls returned from school during the midday break, went straight into the kitchen to help make a huge pile of *rotlis* and, after lunch, scrubbed the pans, before returning to school for the afternoon. Typically, the boys did nothing to help. After Bapuji and the boys had eaten at a table in the front room, served by the girls, all the females ate in the kitchen on the floor sitting on low stools. In earlier years, when my husband was at school and the parents could not afford shoes for all, it was he, the son, who had shoes whilst the girls went barefoot to school.

Ba was unique in her treatment of me. Because she knew I had never done so in my father's house (where I had grown up with not one but six servants to do my every bidding) she wouldn't let me scrub or do any housework. This caused much resentment on the part of my sisters-in-law, the youngest two of whom were still at home. Even so, I was still grateful that my family was too far to see what I had come down to, lower than the standard of living of our servants back home.

When Ba and Bapuji went out they made such an

incongruous couple. She walked several steps behind him, shuffling along to keep pace. Bapuji was, however, a rather mild-natured man and I do believe it was Ba who made the decisions and ruled the roost. Ba was very self-conscious of her poor looks and took great trouble to improve them. She smothered her face with talcum powder to make herself fair (Indians lay great store by fair skin). She used lipstick, quite unheard of in the Gujarati community and severely frowned upon. Whatever the town thought of Ba (and much maligned she certainly was though totally undeservedly) she was very kind to me. She taught me a lot of things useful and practical. She had definite and strong views about child-rearing and other topics. Although she was a pure Vegetarian she believed that eggs were "good for you" and encouraged me to give the children lots of eggs in their diet.

Another wonderful thing she taught me, in those days before baby-walkers and other aids were available, was to sit a baby in a *sufuria* (enormous saucepan) padded on all sides with cushions or small duvets at an age when the baby was not quite steady and was just learning to sit. Baby would be very comfortable but also, more importantly, safe. One could also place the *sufuria* anywhere within sight and keep an eye on the baby.

According to their custom, when in the presence

of my father-in-law, I had to cover my head, right down to my eyes. 'In the presence of my father-in-law' meant, in practice, passing through a room where he might be sitting. I never stayed in the same room and never ever spoke to him or he to me. If he had anything to say to me, he would either shout loud enough for me to hear or tell his wife who would then tell me. What a palaver!

Bapuji (1950)

Ba (1950)

Shobha, Kishore, Reethah and Malini in Raskazone Park (1963)

Kishore, Ashok, Shobha, Mimi, Malini, Reethah in Raskazone Park (1963)

Addressing Others

Husbands and wives didn't address each other by name. They just said what they had to say hoping for the best. If in doubt it was followed by "have you heard?" They did not use their spouse's name when talking to others either. When a man spoke to another man he would refer to the other's wife as "my sister" and his own as "your sister". Similarly, a woman talking to another woman would refer to the other's husband as "my brother" and her own as "your brother". This caused a rumpus once in an office when an Indian clerk got news that his wife was ill and was asked to come home. He went to his English boss for permission to go home. "Sir, can I please go home? Your sister is not well." The Boss was furious. "What have you got to do with my sister?!".

Except for an older person addressing a younger one, nobody called each other just by name. The addressee's name was followed by *-bhai* or *-ben* (brother or sister) for a man or woman of the same age group. For an older person, "uncle" or "aunt" was used, whilst "grandpa" or "grandma" was standard for a person old enough to be their grandparent. This system does have advantages. If you don't know someone's name you just call them by the title. Another man's wife is simply addressed as *bhabhi* (brother's wife). A married woman must treat her in-laws with great respect. That includes her husband's siblings, who must be addressed using their name followed by *-bhai* or *-ben*, even if they are very much younger than herself as was my case. The husband's side of the family is given much respect by the wife's family, but not the other way round; all these rules I learnt. My husband's culture was so alien to me.

A charming custom Gujaratis have is known as *Rakhshabandan*. On this day, every sister ties a *rakhi* to the right wrist of her brothers. A *rakhi* is a wrist band which has evolved into very fancy designs, some quite garish and glitzy. The brother, in return, gives her (you guessed it!) some money. A 'brother' is not necessarily a male child of your own parents. Any man a woman considers a brother – a good friend or a man from the same village – for example, can be 'made' a brother simply by tying a *rakhi*. This is a binding relationship taken very seriously. A woman, for example, could never marry or even flirt with a man she has *rakhi*'d. There is also another tradition, *Bhai-Bees* (brothers-sisters), a day when a sister invites a brother to her home and cooks him a festive meal. Interestingly, I don't know a festival when a woman is honoured in any way.

* * *

It was during that first week in Africa that I learnt my first words of Kiswahili. A man called Juma (literally "Friday") came to meet me. He was the family's handyman. Or perhaps I should call him indispensable man. Tall and well-built, his perfect gleaming teeth added to his charming smile. Juma was always cheerful, a boost to my sagging morale.

"*Jambo, Mama*", he said. I was told the response.

"*Jambo,* Juma."

"*Habari*?" (literally, "news?", but in the sense of "what's your news?")

"*Mzuri*" (good).

This is the standard greeting and response when you meet. The rest, of course, I couldn't understand, but for now I thought the start was very exciting.

Juma came every other day, to do any odd jobs and carry out errands. He had been working for the family for years and I was saddened to note that although they were pleasant to him and even gave him food to take home, they didn't really trust him. There was always a mistrust from the Indians towards the Africans and one took it for granted that every black man was dishonest. This went against the grain for me. Back home where I grew up – in Goa on the east coast of India – everything in the house was left exposed and no servant ever filched the smallest item. Did the distrust of the Africans by Indians push them into dishonesty, or was dishonesty the cause of the distrust? I did feel responsible and ashamed for my ethnic group and the way they interacted with and treated Africans. It said more to me about my people than theirs.

Tanga to Kampala

After the short break staying with Ashok's parents it was time to take off for Kampala, Uganda, to join him. This was a very long journey by train so we were going to have a break at Nairobi, Kenya, with Ashok's sister Sushila. Bapuji had organised transport to the station, once again the Bohora friends to the rescue. He had booked the ticket and meals for the way: lunch, dinner, and breakfast the next morning. Both Bapuji and Ba accompanied me to the station. It would have been very awkward for him to be alone with me.

Our coupé on the train was very comfortable and baby M and I soon settled down. I had brought books to read and pass the time and baby M, lulled by the monotonous rhythm of the train, slept a great deal. I couldn't leave the baby alone in the cabin and it wasn't comfortable to carry her to the dining carriage, so my meals were brought to the cabin. I was very impressed with the service; the compartment was clean, the steward's uniform spotless, and the delicious meals served efficiently. With nothing to do, I had a nap and relaxed both from the trials left behind and in anticipation of what lay ahead. In the evening the Steward appeared again to 'make the bed' which merely involved turning down the back of the seat to reveal a beautifully made bed with spotless sheets, a blanket and a pillow. I was truly impressed with the service of the East African Railways. Later, the Steward brought my dinner which, again, did not disappoint. I had a blissful night, like my baby, lulled by the rhythm of the train.

In the morning, after breakfast, we arrived in Nairobi, Kenya. Sushila's husband Ravind was there to receive us and take us home. Great fuss was made over my Malini and I made equal fuss over their Sandhya who was eight months older. After I was settled Sushila suddenly went into a rage. She took my baby who was wearing pretty baby-bangles given by a friend and screamed "What is this rubbish?! Babies shouldn't be wearing bangles!" She snatched the bangles from my baby's hands and flung them on the floor. I was quite outraged by her behaviour but that was only the beginning. I had to get used to her moods and unpleasantness over the years. The next day I found the same bangles on the hands of Sushila's own baby.

When we were due to leave India, Ashok had written to Sushila (who, he said, was his favourite sister) and asked whether she wanted anything from Bombay. She had asked for three saris for which she would pay. He had told me "Let's give her one as our present." When I was going to Nairobi he asked me to tell her one of the saris was our gift, but, in fact, he charged her for three saris and said it was the price of two, which meant she paid for her own present. That was the first of countless bombshells that revealed to me Ashok's true character.

Sushila said she would take me shopping. When I got ready and appeared before her, she shouted indignantly "where do you think you are going wearing jewellery and carrying a handbag? To a party? You can't go shopping like that, your bag will be snatched in no time. Leave all your jewellery behind, and your handbag too. Roll up some money into a tight parcel and put it inside your bra." I did what I was told, thinking she could have warned me in a more pleasant manner especially as I was not used to the local conditions and dangers. We went to River Road, the shopping area, by car, with our two babies.

Every time we wanted to go into a shop Sushila locked the babies in the car. In retrospect I'm horrified at the thought that we left two young babies locked in a car. If it were today and in England we would probably be prosecuted for child neglect. But crime, especially theft, was so rampant in East Africa and especially in a large city like Nairobi, that it was in fact sensible to lock up children, though I think it would have been more sensible not to have taken the children at all. There were many incidents when women standing on the pavement in the city had their gold chains or handbags snatched by thieves. It was no use chasing them because you would be led into a very narrow lane and sat upon by their accomplices. Once, Sushila's house was burgled during the day when she and Ravind were away at work. Her mother-in-law was gagged and tied to a chair and that was how they found her on return from work several hours later, besides a lot of valuables gone.

Ravind and Sushila took me to a Safari Park which is not far from Nairobi. I thoroughly enjoyed seeing so many African animals for the first time. I almost forgave her all her unkindness to me, until our return home when she said "now you can't say I haven't taken you anywhere". To be truthful, I had not expected her to take me anywhere and would have been content staying at home and treated with kindness. Now it was clear she only took me places either so I couldn't complain or so she could boast of her goodness to me.

Gujaratis make a variety of breads, one of them is called *puris*. Small balls of dough rolled individually into circles and deep fried. Rolling them into perfect circles is an art and takes practice. Being a novice mine never turned out quite round. I remember Sushila shouting at me "Make them round, not maps of India!" By the time it was time to move on I was glad to leave their home and head for Kampala, Uganda.

Ashok came to receive us at the station and took us to our new home for the next four months. I was terrified of African servants after having heard of gruesome incidents of massacres and burglaries and the use of *pangas* (long, sharp knives that could cut you in two with a swipe), especially as I still had difficulty communicating. Ashok had rented a small one-bedroom flat whose upkeep I could cope with without help. Ashok was a Junior Doctor at Mulago Hospital and as such often worked nights and all day. It was lonely but I threw myself into my role of mother and housewife and when baby M slept I learnt Kiswahili from a book I have to this day entitled "Teach Yourself Kiswahili".

A Lesson in Kiswahili

Kiswahili is a fascinating language. Once you learn the rules it is easier than English to a foreign beginner because everything agrees with everything else in a sentence. An interesting fact about the language is that there is a root to a word, as in most other languages, but the changes made to the root are always at the beginning, that is, they are prefixes. "Chair" is *kiti*, "one" is *moja*and "small" is *dogo*. Thus "one small chair" is *kiti kimoja kidogo*. But "chairs" is *viti*, so "three small chairs" is *viti vitatu vidogo*. Words are pronounced as written and written as pronounced. Foreign words such as names usually end in "i":

David becomes Davidi
Paul is Pauli
Thomas is Thomasi

Some foreign adopted nouns:

Shirt is *shati*
cupboard is *kabati*
bicycle is *baiskeli*
bus is *basi*

Some examples of everyday sentences:

I am going to the market = *ninakwenda sokoni*

He ate food = alikula chakula

We shall read the book = *tutasoma kitabu*

Children go to school = *watoto wanakwenda shule*

Some proverbs:

Haba na haba hujaza kibaba = little by little fills the measure

Haraka haraka haina baraka = haste is waste

This is real Kiswahili which I tried to learn from Teach Yourself Kiswahili when Malini was between one and four months old and the only time in my years in Africa when I did not work. The language spoken to Africans by the Indian Community we called "kitchen Swahili". Housewives learnt the words necessary to run their household, things like: crockery, cutlery, kitchen utensils, items of furniture, and so on, plus a few adjectives like good, bad, big, small, thrown in for good measure. There was a smattering of Gujarati words which were combined with the Swahili using no grammar at all. Amazingly, they were well understood, and the credit goes, not to them, but to the clever servants who quickly learnt this corrupt new language. I think it is an insult to a language to speak it badly because one can't be bothered to do better. I took pride in learning it properly but had to do it all on my own as there was no teacher. Still, in spite of my efforts, I sometimes made funny mistakes and thankfully never insulted anyone by using a wrong word… almost.

Soon after Independence I was attending a function with a lot of dignitaries and their wives. Chatting with a group of women, I said to them "I'm a Citizen of Tanzania" (or so I thought). Instantly, and in unison, their jaws dropped and there was a look of horror on their faces. I realised, of course, I had said something wrong and repeated myself in English. They all burst out laughing. What I had said was "I am the President of Tanzania!"President is "*raisi*" whilst citizen is "*raia*". Boy, was I glad I didn't try to show off my Kiswahili when I had the privilege to talk to and shake hands with the President at the time, Julius Nyerere. A great man and a rare politician, Nyerere truly cared for his country and his people and never attempted to line his own pockets. If only his example were followed by politicians all over the world today, things would be very different indeed.

TANZANIAN NATIONAL ANTHEM

Mungu ibariki Afrika
God bless Africa
Wabariki Viongozi wake
Bless its Leaders
Hakima, Umoja na Amani
Wisdom, Unity and Peace
Hizi ni ngao zetu
These are our shields
Afrika na watu wake
Africa and its people.

CHORUS
Ibariki Afrika, ibariki Afrika
Bless Africa, bless Africa.

Mungu ibariki Tanzania
God bless Tanzania
Dumisha uhuru na Umoja
Grant eternal Freedom and Unity
Wake kwa Waume na Watoto
To its Women, Men and Children
Mungu ibariki Tanzania na watu wake
God bless Tanzania and its People.

CHORUS
Ibariki Tanzania, ibariki Tanzania

God bless Tanzania, God bless Tanzania
Tubariki Watoto wa Tanzania
Bless us, the Children of Tanzania.

This anthem moved me deeply then and it still does now. I felt proud of the freedom of my new country, having thrown off the shackles of colonialism during which time anybody non-British was a second class citizen.

Jinja

To help me settle down in Africa, Ashok took us to his *kaka* (paternal uncle) in Jinja some 50 miles from Kampala. Kaka and Kaki had lived there well over 40 years. Jinja was famous for its cotton ginneries and Kaka worked as a Manager in one of them. As soon as we arrived in his presence I covered my head and bent down to touch his feet. He was most amused and laughed. "No, no, no" he protested. "No need to cover your head or touch my feet. You sit with me, eat with me and be a daughter to me." He helped me to my feet. Kaki too was very warm in her welcome. They soon made me feel very much at home and very loved.

Kaka had two brothers. The eldest, in India, had 12 children. The youngest, my Father-in-law Bapuji, had 10. Sadly, Kaka and Kaki had no children. They would have made such wonderful parents. Unlike my father-in-law who, according to old-fashioned custom, would not talk to me at all, Kaka was modern and insisted I sat in the living-room with them and chatted with me as an equal. I had a most interesting and enjoyable three weeks with them.

They had an old man for a houseboy. He had, in

fact, grown old with them, having worked in their house for some 40 years. He was known simply as *mze* (old man) which Kaki pronounced as "maj-eh". On my first day I forgot my watch in the bathroom and Kaki found it there. She gently admonished me for being careless. She said in Africa you take it for granted that your servants are thieves and everything is kept under lock and key or carefully guarded. Mze had never in all those years pilfered anything at all. But the prejudice was so strong, even a kind soul like Kaki couldn't be persuaded that not all Africans were thieves. I was saddened at this attitude and realised that if it hadn't changed in 40 years of faithful and faultless service from Mze, it would never change. Mze was a good and loyal servant. He started work with Kaka as a young man and died in their service never having gained their full trust.

Kaka had an old banger in which he took baby M and me around. He drove, I guessed, at 10mph, either because he was afraid to drive any faster, or because the old banger could not do any better; I never found out. His work took him to neighbouring towns. On those occasions the office gave him a chauffeur-driven Pontiac or a Cadillac. He took baby and me and we travelled in great comfort and luxury. We stayed overnight in a *dak* bungalow (a travellers' rest house, originally found on postal service relay runner routes) which had all the comforts and I felt quite spoilt.

Once we visited a relative who lived in Mbale where he had to go on duty. The husband and his male friends had learnt to eat chicken which they greatly relished. The wife stayed strictly vegetarian but cooked chicken every weekend for the men. Of course she never tasted the non-vegetarian food she cooked but the time I ate there it was delicious. I thought it was very brave of her to cook non-vegetarian. This auntie taught me to make *gulab jamun*: a popular sweet made from thick dried milk powder. I still have the recipe after 50 years but the type of dried milk used is not available in England where I now live so I make it from a packet but never fail to remember that Auntie when I do.

That couple had only one child: a daughter whom they sent to England for further education. She shared a flat with other students from East Africa. One day, whilst they were all playing cards to pass the time, she went to wash her hair in the bathroom. After some time they realised she was gone a long time and went to investigate. There was no response and they then had to force entry and found her dead, overcome by fumes from the boiler. The parents never recovered from the tragic loss of their only child.

Kaka and Kaki (1960)

We Arrive in Tanga

It was in early July 1959 that Ashok and I, with six month old baby M, arrived in Tanga where my parents-in-law had lived 25 years and where Ashok had lived as a little boy and gone to school.

It was hot and humid and little M was intensely distressed once again. I didn't feel too well either, what with the heat, caring for the baby, beginning a cough and wheeze. Most of all, however, was the anxiety about our future in this town as general practitioners and my own personal coping with the in-laws and Gujarati way of life. Ashok reassured me we would do just fine and everyone was eagerly waiting for the new doctors. What this meant, as I later discovered, was that the residents of Tanga wanted to see how much cleverer we might be than the doctors already there. Doctors who were tried, tested and failed in their opinion.

The town had a population of 50,000 with only seven doctors (and of whom only a single one was female) and no others at all within a 60 mile radius. Traffic was so quiet, not a single set of traffic lights in the town. There were a great many sisal plantations in the area and one-fifth of the world's sisal was grown in Tanga province back then.

I was very keen to fit in with my in-laws' customs and live up to their expectations. I had learnt quite a bit as well as some of the Gujarati language, and so it was that as we arrived, Ashok went first to greet his parents who touched his head in blessing. He is not the sort to bend down his head to anyone, much less touch their feet, so his short Mother had to stretch up to touch his head. I don't think it mattered to Ashok whether his parents touched his head or not, he always felt superior to everyone else, especially a woman, whoever she might be. Then came my turn. As I entered the house I took care to cover my head with the pallow of my sari, kept my head low and bent down to touch the feet of each of my parents-in-law. Having touched their feet with both my hands I then touched my chest. They, in turn, each touched my head and Ba made a token gesture of lifting me up to standing. It was not right or fitting for me to look up at my father-in-law, or talk to him, or bare my head in his presence. All this was very new to me but I didn't mind it at all. If anything I thought it very interesting and wanted to know more about their customs.

Ashok stayed in the front room with Bapuji whilst Ba took Malini in her arms and gently guided me to the kitchen where we sat on very low stools about 2" high. These are commonly used as they ate on the floor off a large steel dish called a *thali* and worked at floor level, cooking on a Primus stove or wood fire, preparing the meals squatting on the little stools like my servants did back home. I soon got used to it but was always grateful my folks couldn't see me behave this way. Ba got busy pumping the stove to make masala tea while I, in typical Gujarati style, lifted my sari blouse to bare a breast, covered the breast and the baby with the pallow and nursed her while talking to Ba.

I loved Ba's masala tea and the many other delicacies she cooked and these helped develop the affectionate and comfortable relationship we shared. Bapuji had got the house across the street ready for us to occupy and so, for the next few months, we ate with Ba but slept in the house opposite in the back portion whilst using the front room as our surgery. We had had plans and hopes to go to England for a post-graduate degree like most of our colleagues. Tanganyika, as it was then, was a British colony and Britain was typically considered the best place to study. Unlike our colleagues, however, we had a very young baby; we couldn't take a 6 month old baby along and work in a hospital, nor could we leave a baby behind for a length of time. Because of this we decided to go into practice for a year or 2 before going to the U.K. I'd always loved working in the lab and with micro-life and my own dream was to specialise in Bacteriology. In fact, if I hadn't done medicine I would surely have studied Microbiology.

Word quickly spread around Tanga that we intended to start our own practice and soon there were offers of premises. We were informed about a place in *Bara Bara Saba* (7th street) that might be suitable. And so it was that on a hot July day we had gone to inspect a house in the *Ngamiani* ("of the camels") area of Tanga. The inhabitants here were mostly African and Arab with a sprinkling of Indian merchants. The place looked promising, rooms were large and recently painted and it was well situated on the corner of *Bara Bara Saba.*

My First Patient

We were discussing the pros and cons of the house as a surgery when suddenly there was a screech of brakes in front of the house and a middle-aged Arab in long white robes dashed in looking for *Mama Mganga*. He wanted me to come straightaway to deliver his wife's 13th child. She had started pains. He kept saying "*Haraka, Haraka*!", which was duly translated to me as "Hurry, Hurry". My Kiswahili was still poor as I had had no practice speaking it. I had no tools with me required for a delivery, but that didn't worry the man. Ashok explained the situation but the man was adamant. He said he would give me all that was required. "I'll give you scissors and thread, you just come", he insisted, and as I rushed with him to his van, Ashok very quickly told me the words for scissors and thread. I had no time to think what I might do if there was any complication such as excessive bleeding (quite common after multiple deliveries), or need to resuscitate the baby.

We sped off in his van to the edge of the town to a little whitewashed, thatched house typical of the Arab and African homes, and with a cemented veranda. I had been repeating the words for scissors and thread all the way. The Arab rushed into his shop and came out with an ice-cold Fanta to refresh me before I could get to work. It was a bright, sunny day. He ushered me in and I suddenly found myself, having come in from the bright tropical sun outside, in total darkness, unable to adjust my eyes.

The one little high window had been covered with sackcloth to exclude the light. I could not even see the outline of my patient let alone her business end. As my eyes adjusted to the darkness, I could make out a large 4-poster bed in one corner. But all the sounds came from the floor. I went towards the bed and realised it was not occupied. So where was my patient? An old woman appeared and led me to her. Quite sensibly, to save messing up the bed, the Arabs put sackcloths on the floor, and that's where my patient lay, on the floor on a pile of jute sackcloths. Two old women were squatted on either side of her, talking gently to soothe her or chanting magic spells, I could not tell. Apart from a case of first-aid I had never attended to a patient on the floor. Now there I was, dressed in a sari delivering an Arab baby on the floor on gunny-bags. There was no sound at first but then I heard a little groan. Very unusual at a delivery; I had been used to hearing women screaming during their deliveries, either imploring heavenly help or cursing the man who had put them in that predicament.

But then all my previous patients had been Indians. One little groan came out of this Arab patient and at once the husband was at the door. "Must you make so much noise? The whole neighbourhood will know you are having a baby, one would think nobody has ever given birth to a baby before!" He didn't mean to be unkind but an Arab woman is expected to be truly stoic. I was to find out in the following months and years just how much. She was ready to push and in no time and without any fuss and even less noise on the part of the mother, we had a howling baby boy in all the mess on gunny-bags

I asked the old woman for the thread and scissors, having repeated the words all through the drive to memorise them. I was handed scissors and thick thread with which I tied the cord and separated the baby. One of the old women took the baby while the other massaged Khadija's tummy and the placenta was out. No undue bleeding, thank goodness. It was my good luck that thread and scissors was all I needed for this delivery. The old women and the patient between them did everything. When the afterbirth was out and she had been cleaned, Khadija, without fuss, got up and went to lie on the bed. Grandma took charge of the infant. By now I could see somewhat clearly round the room. I guess my patient could not have been over 35 years old but she looked 60. To have borne 13 children by the age of 35! How different her experiences of life had been from mine. She had tattoo marks all over her forehead, cheeks and chin in a delicate pattern of lines and dots. I thought she looked beautiful and I was overwhelmed by her strength and courage.

When I had finished and come out of the room onto the verandah, the husband was waiting for me with another bottle of ice-cold Fanta from his shop and insisted I refresh myself before he took me back. I visited Khadija daily for the next few days. She never had a complaint. No backaches, no headaches, no problems of any sort, complained of by my earlier patients. On the 10th day the husband came to my surgery with the payment and a gift for me. Khadija went on to have two more pregnancies, one of which miscarried. I presided both times.

Beginnings

We settled very quickly into our *Bara Bara Saba* surgery. All of Tanga seemed to have heard of us and people thronged to 'see' and consult us for a variety of reasons. Not that they thought we were particularly clever and worth consulting.

The first Indian woman who visited me started by saying "I have tried all the doctors in this town and they are all useless. Now let us see how clever you are." Needless to say my treatment was not successful either; she was determined and had come with her mind already made up that I would be as useless as all the other doctors in town. Bad luck to her, no new doctor came to the town after us for her to put to the test. So she was stuck with a load of useless doctors all competing in uselessness. An Indian man came to see Ashok. He had unpaid bills with all the other doctors. He was trying to kill time before someone took him to Court. Another Indian man said to Ashok "I heard you have a Certificate from Bombay University. Dr X trained in Y; it doesn't have a great reputation." One Indian woman said "I go to Dr Shankar (the other female doctor in the town) but she is in India visiting relatives so I had to come to you." This sort of disdain was rife amongst the Gujaratis.

The Arab and African patients, though, were a delight. They had such faith in the Doctor, it made it all worthwhile. Some Arabs had *dukas* (small shops) out in the country. Because of the incredibly low density of medical practitioners in the area they would travel long distances. Arab men liked a woman doctor to attend to their womenfolk and children. As they had up to 4 wives and innumerable children they kept us busy. It took them several hours on rough roads to reach our town. Sometimes they arrived at 8pm on a Sunday or even later when surgery was closed and we were trying to relax. They turned up at the house with a child running high temperature or a wife with severe abdominal pain. How can you turn away someone who has come all those miles because they are so ill and have such faith in you?

We had a lot of Arab patients in the town too. The family I remember best was that of two brothers, Mbarak and Saíd, their wives, children, a widowed mother and a widowed aunt. There was also an old man around, probably an impoverished relative. The Arabs were my favourite patients. They had great faith, affection and respect and I was fond of them. They also always paid cash and promptly.

African patients too were very rewarding to treat.

They too came because they had faith in you, not to test you. I do believe a rapport and trust between doctor and patient is essential to healing. This one reason made it impossible for me to ever succeed in treating a Gujarati patient.

To boost our income in the beginning we started going to a small town called Pangani, further up the coast. Once a week we would gather our wares, drive up and set up clinic in a small house. We did well as there were no doctors in town. We made an outing of it and the young in-laws came with us. They tried to help. Once, my brother-in-law Yash was standing by when I was testing a Patient's blood pressure. At the sight of the cuff being pumped up he simply passed out. Some help!

The Gujaratis, when parting, used to say "*Bas*!", which they anglicised into "okay!", which in turn was 'Swahili-ised' into "*haya*!". When we first went to Pangani we met a lot of people and my husband shook hands with the men on parting and said "*Haya*!" to each. I didn't hear correctly and, as I wished each person, said "*Hi, hi*!" taking it for granted that most words are a repeated syllable in Swahili. They must have thought this rather strange.

Ashok and Mimi (1963)

Joys and Sorrows of Doctoring

A *kanga* is an item of clothing with many uses. It comes as a pair of rectangles of fabric, each about 60" x 35" (150 x 90cm). One of the pieces is wrapped round a woman's waist or above the bust and tucked in; the other piece goes above the shoulders, on the head as a turban, rolled to form a cushion to carry weights on the head, or as a sling to carry goods or a baby as she went about her daily tasks. The baby was on her hip if she was walking, on her back for walking or bending in the fields, quite comfortable and safe in close contact with the mother. Alternatively, she could easily swing the baby round to the front for breast-feeding which she did whether she was walking, working or just sitting. She carried the baby in this close body contact and suckled it for the first two years of its life. I noted a close bond between my adult patients, male or female, and their mothers. I do believe those bonds were forged from the carrying in close contact through babyhood.

Kangas originated in the mid-19th century on the coast of East Africa when women in Zanzibar bought scarves from the Portuguese. These came as a continuous bale of cotton material which was cut into (nec)kerchiefs. These evolved into *kangas* by joining kerchiefs together. Originally, the print was dark with white spots and this gave it the name, *kanga*, which means guinea-fowl. Nowadays, *kangas* have a bold central area and a wide border all round. They also have printed proverbs and sayings and are very colourful. *Kangas* are 100% cotton and hence are very cool and soft. My own children as babies were always carried in a *kanga* sling by the *ayah*.

And what about the fathers? Muslim men can have up to four wives at any one time, and many of our patients did. A Muslim man can also divorce his wife by simply saying the words "*Talak, talak, talak*" upon which she is then as free as he is. I don't know that all the couples that came to us were actually married, but there never seemed to be a problem like court cases and wrangles over alimony. Children stayed with mother and, however many fathers there might have been to a woman's children, the respective father never failed his obligations to his children. And so it was that if a child was ill and needed to go to the doctors, the mother informed the respective father and he either took the child himself or gave the money for the fee to the mother. Or quite often the current co-habitee would pay for any of the children, whether his or not.

When a man had more than one wife they often lived all under the same roof. Again, there did not seem to be any rivalry. The eldest was happy because she had the status of senior wife and was given the respect due to her by the others. The youngest was the current favourite; that and her youth were enough to give her happiness. The middle ones were also satisfied; after all, they were fed, clothed and had a roof over their heads. They had children and these were cared for and they had the comfort of shared parental responsibilities. Never a problem with baby-sitting!

If a man had two wives, each looked after the other's children besides her own. Once I asked a woman who had brought a child to the surgery "is this your child?" to which she replied "*mtoto ya menzangu*" (my friend's child). I came to learn that this meant "it's the child of my husband's other wife". The "friend" was a co-wife. There was no bitterness in this – just a factual statement. She treated the child as if it were her own. As relationships formed and broke, children had no end of half-siblings. It felt strange when someone said "this is my brother, <u>one</u> mother and <u>one</u> father", stressing the "one" with pride.

* * *

Just like the Arabs, Africans gave a woman doctor tremendous respect and preferred a *mama mganga* for their women and children. As such I had a very good clientele and enjoyed treating them very much.

Lamu lies in Kenya somewhere north of where we were in Tanzania. A lot of men from Lamu came to Tanga on business. They often came for treatment but we rarely saw their women.

Old Ibrahim Rasool looked an old man but was probably younger than he looked, probably sixty. He would drop in to consult Ashok every time he was in Tanga either for a problem of his own or to get medicine to take home for a family member. Whether our long-distance diagnoses and treatments worked I shall never know but as the fringe Arabs came again and again I guess they did.

On one occasion Ibrahim brought his youngest wife, about 20 years old, with the complaint that she was not conceiving. He had been married to Safira for 2 years. On questioning it transpired that Ibrahim had had 17 wives (not all at the same time) in his lifetime, but not one had given him a child. Several of them had had children before he had married them or by other husbands after he divorced them. But it never once occurred to old Ibrahim that the fault might lie with him as it proved to be.

I examined the wife. She was in her twenties, very healthy and clinically there was nothing amiss. Ashok had to tactfully break the news to Ibrahim as to what was amiss. Ibrahim insisted on an injection that would improve his prowess. I have no idea what Ashok gave him. About 18 months later he came with the wife and a baby. We could only guess where a pretty young wife of an old sterile man got the baby from. In this story I think they really lived happily ever after.

I shall always remember old Ibrahim's wise words when someone mentioned a "holy day and propitious time". He said "Every day is a holy day, every day is God's day." In his own way he echoed my belief that one's day is good or bad depending on how one uses it and learns from it.

Old Ibrahim was a righteous man and, cheat or no cheat, deserved the joy of being a father.

Now and then we would have a Masai for a patient as they live mostly in the interior of Tanzania. They kept very much to themselves and looked rather suspiciously at others. They carried themselves tall and proud and looked very regal and handsome in their hairstyles and the colourful *shuka* (blanket) they wore. When I saw my very first Masai patient I asked "what's the problem?" in Swahili, only to be abruptly answered "you should know; <u>you</u> are the doctor". He wasn't very forthcoming with information which I had to tactfully collect by indirect questions. He obviously believed that a doctor was a magician and could just look at a person and make a diagnosis. I learnt my lesson on how to tackle this variety of patient. As soon as greetings were over, I would make the patient lie on the couch and start examining from top to toe while asking questions as to where it hurt, or, if a child, did it pass worms, etcetera.

My instruments like blood pressure apparatus, stethoscope, otoscope were a great help in impressing them with my knowledge and wisdom and, dare I say it, wizardry? Sticking a needle expertly into the flesh also worked miracles. I was awfully grateful to discover how easy it was to please and to cure my African and Arab patients. They came invariably with curable problems and real physical ailments. No psycho-somatic complaints which abound in the West. They had such faith in the doctor that a *sindano* (hypodermic syringe) was enough to cure any ailment, big or small. Usually they got better and the doctor was praised. When things didn't get better and a patient got worse or died, which is inevitable in any practice at some point, it was Allah's will.

My experience in the Gujarati community was quite the opposite. Patients never got better, were never grateful, and there was never a word of thanks even for attending promptly in the middle of the night. Had I been non-Indian myself I guess things would have been different. But just being Indian caused a lot of jealousy and a need to prove me wrong all the time. I had to be on guard every minute with every word or gesture I made. Considering that

I wasn't used to their way of life it was incredibly difficult and I don't think I ever succeeded in winning them over. One can't work well or enjoy working without good rapport with a patient.

All Gujaratis without exception were either merchants themselves or were members of a merchant family. The only values they knew were measured in shillings and cents. They treated me as if I were inferior in the doctor-patient transaction because <u>they</u> would be paying <u>me</u> for this transaction. Just as they walked into a shop and talked to the shopkeeper as if they were their inferior. They would categorically tell them "that's too much, I'll pay you this much." There was no: "Would you reduce the price?" The attitude was "I am the boss (even if it is your shop)".The shopkeeper haggled a bit but in the end gave some discount. "okay, *Nanubhai*, as you are an old friend of my brother-in-law's, I'll give you 10% discount." Or the buyer might be the neighbour of the shopkeeper's cousin, or the teacher of their child, or their ancestors came from the same village in India…

There was always some reason to give a discount and also save face at the same time. So why should they not get a discount from the doctor? All our African and Arab patients paid cash. In all those years in Tanga we never had a problem with them. Not so the Gujaratis. They visited the surgery or we visited in their homes; an account was kept and a bill sent at the end of the month. No payment. Next month a reminder. No response. After 3 months we sent a strong reminder with threat of court action. Mr Patel turned up at the surgery waving the bill in the air. "The hardware shop gives me 15% discount. What are you going to give me?"

Ashok answered "I'm not a hardware merchant, I'm a Doctor. Your payment is three months overdue. The interest on this amount for three months is…" Mr Patel took out a thick wad of notes from his pocket and paid the bill in cash. We were not always that lucky. There were occasions when we did take someone to court. They had not attended again because they rotated from doctor to doctor playing Musical Doctors. This month they were probably sitting in Dr Sirvan's chair, or that of Dr Karim, Dr Sekana or Dr Dilan. But we couldn't remove our chair and consider them out of the game because that would not be ethical. I never felt a given family were my patients with whom I could build a rapport, have mutual respect and develop a certain degree of affection. I was there to be used and abused. They were there to make sure I would not succeed.

Goa

My ancestors some 400 years ago were Hindu Brahmans in Goa. One day, Portuguese explorer Vasco Da Gama arrived from Portugal and 'discovered the Indies', changing my ancestors' destinies forever in the process. Hot on the heels of the Portuguese came the missionaries, among them the Spanish Jesuit Francis Xavier, and they transformed our lives further and irreversibly by converting us to Catholicism. This they did by preaching, giving rice and other foods, and by polluting our water wells with meat so those who drank from those wells could no longer be accepted by their community. Had the Portuguese not arrived, converted and colonised, I wonder what the course of our history and our destiny might have been. But that question is purely academic.

They came, they conquered, they baptised. Surnames such as D'Souza, Fernandes, Da Costa, Pereira, and first names like Maria, João, José, Teresa and Luis. At the time of my childhood there seemed to be a fashion for Greek names – Sócrates, Aristotle, Theophilos, Eleutherio, Euclid, Pantaleon, Serapeon – though don't ask me why. Though these names amused and fascinated me, I was glad we didn't have any such in our family. The one thing the Portuguese could not change because it was too deeply ingrained, was the Caste system. And so we continued to be Brahmans, Shardos and Sudras, besides other tribal castes. As before the conversion, the castes did not mix and did not intermarry.

The Brahmans were the best educated, had the white collar jobs or were professionals or landowners. The Sudras were mainly the servant class, and worked in the fields that belonged to the Brahmans as workers and artisans, skilled or unskilled. The Shardos were an in-between sort of caste and had jobs in-between. They would supervise a coconut harvest or do clerical jobs. The three castes never mixed socially. When a Sudra came to our house they came in from the back entrance. They never sat but always stood in the presence of a Brahman. Our Shardo supervisor ate in our house during a coconut harvest. He sat at a table like us but on his own and ate with his hands like the servants. His food was better than the servants', but not as good as ours. There was another group of people, the tribals or *Kunbis* who were yet another class. They wore distinctive clothes, very colourful, and a lot of jewellery. They did manual jobs but I thought them to be very intelligent. In later years, given the opportunity, they got educated and many became professionals.

Life for us was to change with the independence of the rest of India from the British in 1947, and then of Goa from the Portuguese in 1961 when it integrated with the rest of India. I was born in 1932 into a deeply religious Catholic family of Goan Brahmans – the sixth child of my parents – and was christened Maria Emilia Francisca Correia Afonso. What a mouthful! Maria because every female Catholic child had the Virgin's name as her first name; Emilia after my *mamagrande* (maternal grandmother); Francisca because I was born in the year of one of the many expositions of the body of Spanish missionary St Francis Xavier (which it is believed did not decompose and is still preserved in a silver casket in the cathedral of *Bom Jesus* in Old Goa).

The double surname is an interesting story. My paternal great-grandmother was Propercia Correia whose parents had no sons. According to custom, when a family had no sons, the eldest son-in-law lived in the wife's house (the opposite of the norm), and thus did my great-grandfather, a lawyer, Agostinho Afonso. Their children inherited the surnames of both parents and so from my grandfather on we were all Correia Afonsos. My mother, who had two surnames of her own, ended up having four after marriage as the Portuguese custom was for a married woman to keep her surname and add on her husband's. So it was that my Mother ended up as Olivia Adelina Etelvina Rodrigues Chico Correia Afonso – enough to get one out of breath!

Both my parents' families were highly educated. My papa had a first class degree in Agriculture from the Poona (now Pune) Agricultural College. His name is in an Honours list there. Mama was in the first group of girls to do the matriculation exam in 1916, as well as the first batch of girls to get a BA degree in Baroda, in 1920. Mama spoke only English, having been born and having grown up in British India. Papa's family in Goa spoke only Portuguese, but his brother and he were educated in English which must have made things easier than for Mama's sister whose husband spoke no English and she no Portuguese at all. Her sister's marriage had been arranged and I wonder how they communicated except perhaps in the language of love.

In those days, no man worth his salt, let his wife work, so Mama never did. A Brahman wife didn't work in the house either. I'm sure Mama didn't even know how to make a cup of tea right up to her death at the age of 72 as there were always servants to do her every bidding.

So this was how I grew up, in a large, extremely Catholic, Brahman family, in the lap of luxury – never having to lift a finger to get myself even a glass of water. This was the same for any of the *Okolbai* I mentioned before. Both of her parents-in-law would hug, kiss (on both cheeks as in the Portuguese custom) and mollycoddle her, never letting her exert herself. She had umpteen servants to carry out her every wish. What a contrast to my new life in a Gujarati family!

Siafu and Mango Fly

It happened not long after we arrived in Tanga. We had made friends with a young couple, Manhar and Monisha. They were recently married and had a cosy bungalow by the sea. "Come over for a cup of tea", they had said. So we went with our six month old Malini. Baby fell asleep and I was reluctant to put her on a bed in case she rolled over and fell. "No problem" said Monisha, "I'll make a bed on the floor". She put a *godri* (thin Indian duvet) on the floor and baby was very comfortable. We sat on the verandah enjoying our tea and chat. After a while I went to check on the baby… and just in time. I saw a black patch on the floor moving steadily and with a purpose towards my baby. It was a swarm of ants known locally as *siafu* making a bee-line for Malini. Had I succumbed to another samosa and been a few minutes later… I dread to think of the consequences. Siafu are not poisonous but the bites of hundreds of these ants could be fatal to a baby.

Being new to Africa there was so much I needed to learn and so many lessons I learnt the hard way or by experience alone. When baby M was about nine months and a very healthy baby, one day she gave a sharp and loud screech of pain out of the blue. She was well, there was no sign of illness, no fever. It stopped as sharply as it had started. After a while the episode repeated itself, with a loud screech and obvious pain which stopped just as sharply. The child was well and I was puzzled. But on examination I found a little boil on her leg and the intermittent screeching continued with no other clue. The next day the boil came to a head and, horror of horrors, a little worm popped its very ugly head out of the skin.

Fortunately, my *ayah* was familiar with this situation and squeezed it out. It came out alive and wriggling. I can't express the horror I felt. (An *ayah* is a woman servant who looks after children and all their needs like bathing, washing, ironing, nappy-changing. *Ayahs* carry babies in *kangas.*) I found out it was due to the mango-fly. It bites a human and lays an egg under the skin. The victim feels nothing until the egg hatches and the maggot needs to come out. It bites its way out of the skin which causes the excruciating pain. My poor baby! I only realised how much pain baby M had suffered when a few days later I went through the same experience. The pain really was excruciating. I still have the scar, I learnt later that mango-flies lay several eggs into a human even up to 200. Thankfully, baby M and I only suffered one each.

An Average Day

One day a Gujarati woman in a colourful sari and plenty of jewellery walked into the surgery with head held high and shouted in an imperious tone "Nurse! Nurse!" I came to the door and after greeting her said "I'm not a nurse, I am a doctor". "How can you be a doctor", she said haughtily, "you are a woman. Men are doctors, women are nurses!" I knew she would not believe me but had to tell her. "That may be what you think. But I am a doctor with a doctor's degree." "Hh!", she snarled. "Anyway, my problem is not women's complaint. I'll see the man doctor." The Gujarati woman generally believed that a woman was incapable of understanding and much less treating anything that was not to do with 'women's complaints'. Even after treating these, they would turn up at the surgery waving the bill furiously. "What is this? The Ironmonger gives me 15% discount. What discount are you going to give me?" My husband was quite capable of dealing with them and even taking them to Court, so I left money matters to him.

In the evening when the houseboy had gone home I cooked the evening meal. I used to have all three children in the kitchen at the end away from the cooker. Mal doing homework, Reethah doing drawings which she loved and was very good at, and baby Jay (my thirdborn, rhymes with "sky") in the high chair with baby toys. Where was my husband? Usually at someone else's home telling them how much he loved his wife (as I managed to glean on occasions from conversations with them). Quite often a patient would call at the door. "Mama, I want a *sindano*". That meant he had gonorrhoea and wanted a penicillin injection. Venereal disease, particularly gonorrhoea, was rampant. I once assumed that a male patient would want a male doctor and said "*Bwana mganga* is not in". "But you are *mganga*, aren't you?" He had no qualms about being attended to by a *mama mganga*. I was overwhelmed – ashamed that I had doubted his faith.

* * *

Quick, back into the kitchen; cooker off; kids out of the kitchen; run to the surgery downstairs; attend to the patient; lock up surgery; run upstairs; cooker on; kids back in; finish cooking the meal; feed the children. Later, get them ready, put them to bed, then wait for my wayward husband. Indians are very hospitable and nobody goes away without the offer of a meal. As such, Ashok had often already eaten at someone else's house and on such occasions I ate alone after having waited to eat together. In retrospect, I believe that if I'd been more firm and not so docile in my behaviour towards my husband then perhaps he wouldn't have got away with it, but alas, his behaviour only worsened as time went on. At that point, however, I was so overwhelmed with all my problems that I had no energy to stand up to him.

Doing Your Best

Working in a small town in Tanzania in the 1960s one had to be very resourceful, a jack of all trades. Missionary hospitals, if there was one, were good and quite well stocked and the staff were always and unfailingly caring. But government hospitals (and these were in far greater abundance) were very inefficient and wasteful, whilst their staff were not known for kindness or caring. Little wonder, then, that people didn't want to go to the local hospital. "You only go to hospital to die", was the general consensus, and people would rather die at home with their family around than chance it in hospital.

We had to put our hands to all sorts of medical problems. We delivered babies, did surgery which was not always minor, and even extracted teeth, never having done that in our training. Seeing the need for it, my husband ordered a set of instruments for tooth extraction and got on with it. It was a matter of doing what one could. There was no dentist for hundreds of miles around.

Once, during a visit to London, I bumped into Nadia, a colleague who had emigrated to Malawi and worked in a small hospital out in the bush (in the wild). We exchanged news and experiences. She told me she had even done some brain surgery. It was a question of doing your best with some hope of saving a life or letting your patient die because you did nothing. She said "While the nurses got the patient ready for operation, I went into the next room and quickly read up what I should do. But a lot of it was following gut feelings and doing my best." I was not surprised, knowing the thoroughness of whatever Nadia did and the resilience of the local population that her patient survived the operation only to die a couple of years later of snake-bite.

A woman once walked into the surgery carrying one ear in her hand. Her man had sliced it off in a fit of rage. The ear was stitched back and it took. When Jay was a toddler, the *ayah* put him on the top bunk of a bunk bed. The child rolled over in his sleep and fell, hitting his forehead on the pedestal of a rotating standard fan. He had a big gash on the forehead and was bleeding profusely. In England we would not think twice before taking him to casualty to have stitches given by another doctor, but out there, that moment, we were both parents and doctors. I had to be mother and cuddle, control and soothe the child, whilst my husband was the surgeon and gave the stitches, trying to forget this was his own baby he was stitching.

I was never asked for a visit to an African home.

The Arabs only called me to their homes to deliver their womenfolk. Otherwise they came to the surgery or even my home from any distance away and in any state of health. Visits were asked for only by Indians. Our town of 50,000 people had quiet streets and not a single set of traffic lights. When I had to make a visit while the *ayah* was not in my house to look after little Mal I just took her with me. I drove with her on my lap. I am appalled to think I could ever have done such a thing but at that time and in that place that is what people did and I had no alternative. I am glad to say no harm ever came to the child. How on earth did I manage after I had the other two children?!

* * *

Tuesday, am

Malini has been taken to *motiben* (husband's eldest sister) for the morning as *ayah* has not turned up. It is a lovely day but the heat is already getting hold of my nerves besides the sweat-glands. Nothing quenches thirst like ice water and there is always a big jug full of it. The ice has long melted but the water is still refreshingly cool. I await my first patient of the day while I catch up with medical journals interspersed with sips of water.

"*Hodi*!" I hear my first patient. Maniben Patel walks

in with her 16 year old daughter Neeta in tow. Neeta doesn't look happy to be in a doctor's surgery. It is the mother who relates the girl's complaints. She has been rather listless lately and her monthly periods are not satisfactory or sometimes absent. One could have diagnosed this case just by a look at the girl, she is so pale. Neeta is very anaemic and I advise on diet and prescribe iron and vitamins. The pair leave without paying of course. They have been gone barely a minute when a minor hurricane blows into my surgery in the form of a patient named Sushila Mehta. She has not come in for a consultation. "What's wrong with Maniben's daughter?" she demands. "I saw her coming in here just now". She has a bandage on her right hand, otherwise I imagine she would have banged a fist on the desk to add drama to her demand. "I'm sorry I can't divulge the problems of my patients", I say with as much patience as I can muster. I am livid but must be in control. "She must be pregnant and come to you for an abortion. Why else should a sixteen-year old girl come to a nurse? That's why you don't want to tell, but I know it." I reply as politely as possible: "I am a doctor, not a nurse and my patients' problems are none of your business. So, anything I can do for you?" She stomps out of the surgery and towards the town. I imagine a huge bell in her hand like a town crier, bandage or not. *Tring, tring, tring.* "Oyez, Oyez!

Neeta Patel is pregnant and she is having an abortion done by Nurse D." It was easy to picture Mrs Mehta in a loud whisper to Mrs Shah who would repeat in a slightly louder whisper to Mrs K... on to Mrs A... Mrs B... Mrs Z as they swarmed as an army of bees for the sweet honey of gossip and hot *masala chai.*

* * *

Somabhai's 12-year old boy drops in. "My Father asks you to come quick to see my sister; she is bleeding". I'm there in a flash, my toddler in the hands of Manaisha who has thankfully just arrived. My patient, Sunita, is 19 years old and 32 weeks into her first pregnancy. She had been alright all along but suddenly this morning she had a bout of bleeding. The baby seems okay and on examination I diagnose placenta praevia (when the placenta lies too low in the womb). My mind flashes back to that other case of the condition a few years earlier when I was younger, less experienced and learnt a very hard lesson in obstetrics.

I was a Resident Medical Officer (RMO) at the Noor Hospital, a private Muslim hospital in Bombay. The hospital was well provided and several consultants brought their private patients to it. It had good facilities including a lab and x-ray facilities. There were 2 RMO posts and my colleague Zarina and I got on well and had good nursing support. One Saturday, late in the evening, a woman called Aisha was admitted. She was 36 weeks pregnant and had been having mild pains. The normal procedure would have been to have her blood tests including blood group done on admission. But this being very late on a Saturday this was not done.

Sunday dawned peaceful as usual. Many of the Staff went home to their families. After lunch Zarina left to visit an ailing Aunt and more nurses left, some for the cinema, some for a walk on the sea-front with their boyfriends. I was on duty with a minimal back-up of nurses. All was peace and quiet… but alas, not for long. At about 2.30pm a nurse shouted for me. "Come quick, she is bleeding". Aisha was lying in a big pool of blood, looking deathly pale and her eyes had glazed over. I could not feel her pulse. We carried out the normal procedure and tried to start a drip but couldn't find a vein. I feared young Aisha was slipping away fast. The other junior nurse grabbed the phone and it was our good luck that the consultant was just about leaving her house and was caught in time and the anaesthetist was at home on call. They were both by our side in minutes and between us we managed to get a drip going and get things under control. Aisha recovered and stayed on in hospital till she was delivered at 38 weeks of a healthy baby boy. This case had a happy ending but could have ended in tragedy. It taught me a harsh lesson and I remembered what our obstetrics tutor Dr Sarayia had said about placenta praevia: once diagnosed, the patient should be in hospital or at least within quick reach.

Back to here and now. I withdrew into the living room to discuss the case with Sunita's father. Mother would not leave the girl's side. I advised Mr K that Sunita should be admitted to hospital. I explained placenta praevia and the good chance she might have a big bout of bleeding with serious and dangerous consequences to both mother and baby. Mr K was adamant; "no hospital. If you don't know how to treat my daughter, I will call another doctor who knows better" he said disdainfully. He meant it. I left with my case and no fee for my time. I learnt later that a different Dr D had been summoned. He was a lot older than myself and knew the local people's attitudes and how to handle them. I guess he must have prescribed complete bed rest and given some injection. Sunita went to near full term and had a healthy baby.

I had to reassess my medical training and remembered my tutor again. In those days, in India, so many women died of bleeding either during or immediately after delivery, especially the latter.

"How do you treat a case of post-partum haemorrhage?" (immediately after birth) he had asked. We medical students had come up with various suggestions. He finally summed up.

"If you are in a large, well equipped hospital…

"If you are in a small country hospital, you…

"If you are in the patient's home and can't get her to a hospital…

"If you are in the back of beyond with nothing and no-one to help you, you shred your sari to ribbons and pack the vagina very tightly with your bare hands."

I shall never forget Dr Sarayia's simple and practical wisdom. Doctors trained and practising in the West will never understand the value of that wisdom; they don't need it. But in India in the 1950s, out in little villages miles from the nearest town, the teachings of our medical school were often of no use at all. The practice of medicine is common-sense first, anything else may or may not be useful. Few doctors worked in these conditions. You had to have a truly 'missionary spirit' and no family commitment to be able to work in such places. By far the majority of us have a family to feed and educate, and have no qualms about choosing to practice in a city or town.

Ayahs

When I started work which was very soon after arrival in Tanga, we needed an *ayah* for baby M. We lived across the street from Bapuji and Ba and ate with them so there was no need of a houseboy. A family friend whose little girl had just started school and no longer needed an *ayah* passed hers on to us and so it was that Lucia, a Makonde woman, came to be Malini's first *ayah*. The Makonde tribe live in southern Tanzania and northern Mozambique. They are very talented wood carvers and made exquisite carvings that went all over the world. Some carvings were several feet tall with figures intertwined as if climbing one on top of the next, from bottom to top. I have not seen more interesting or technically difficult carvings anywhere in my travels. The Makonde also have another distinguishing custom. They tattoo their faces, again in exquisite designs, and women pierce their upper lip and fill the hole with a black button about 1cm in diameter. They also file their front teeth into pointed pegs. The Makonde used to be cannibals, I later learnt. People would jokingly ask "Does she have little nibbles at your baby when she is peckish?"

Our Lucia looked beautiful with her tattoos on the cheeks, forehead and chin, the customary black button in the flesh of her upper lip and her flashing smile exhibiting her pointed, well filed teeth. She had been converted to Catholicism at some point. She was honest, clean, extremely loyal and, best of all, she loved my baby; she was utterly devoted to and proud of baby M, as well as being thoroughly reliable. She was simply the best *ayah* we ever had. Malini was quite fair-skinned and a very pretty baby. When Lucia took her out in her pram, she took it as a personal compliment when people admired the baby. She would come home and boast to me about all the compliments that had been paid. People would stop to give her sweets or biscuits and Lucia was proud to report to me that people often asked "*mtoto ya mzungu*?" (is it a European child?) During the months that Lucia was with us I hadn't a care about home or baby. We were both very distraught when she had to leave us to look after her elderly parents in her village. I never saw her again. It was my loss, not hers.

Doing a full-time general practice in Tanzania and looking after your home and children is not humanly possible. Full-time practice in Tanzania meant exactly that; day or night, Sunday afternoon or weekdays at 9pm, there was no saying when there would be a call to visit or a patient might walk into your house. People came to the front door which was always open through the day and called out "*hodi*!" If there was no response they went on shouting "*hodi*" every few steps and walking steadily into the house. Usually the houseboy intercepted them at the door of the kitchen, but sometimes they reached a bedroom. I loved the sound of "*Hodi*! *Hodi*!" and people who lived in East Africa say it to this day in England when they visit one another.

It was absolutely vital to have an *ayah*, a woman to look after the children. *Ayahs* were as unreliable as houseboys in turning up to work and without notice I would often realise at 8am, right at the peak of domestic activity, making and feeding breakfast to husband and children and getting myself ready, that the *ayah* wasn't going to turn up. What do I do now? I can't leave baby at home and I can't just not go to the surgery which by 8.30 am was already getting busy. There was many a time when I dashed for the bottle and feeds and clothes for the day and my handbag, rushed to the nursery in later years or to my sister-in-law to palm my baby off on her and arrived at surgery huffing and puffing. I was indeed fortunate that all my three children turned out to be very healthy and sailed through their measles and mumps without batting an eyelid. I truly could not have coped otherwise. In fact, looking back, I can't believe that I coped even with servants around. My husband's mother and eldest sister were of immeasurable help.

After Lucia we tried three *ayahs* all of whom were dishonest or uncouth before we found Manaisha and her younger sister Margaret who worked for us alternately for several years. Manaisha was a responsible, trustworthy and mature woman, good at her work and fond of the children. She often stayed late to babysit when Ashok and I went to the cinema. Margaret was a most interesting character, pretty and full of fun. She was very popular with the milkman and the vegetable seller who came to the door with their wares and practically every day she had some vegetables or milk to take home and I knew I had not paid for them They would spend ages at our door chatting Margaret up (or she them!) at the expense of business time. How did she repay them for these gifts? I wondered.

The single criterion for the definition of what makes a place one's residence or address is where one sleeps. In Swahili the word for "live" and "sleep" is the same eg "where do you live?" is the same as "where do you sleep?" I knew where Manaisha lived (slept) as we often dropped her home after babysitting. Once I asked her "Where does Margaret sleep?" and she said that "it depends who she is sleeping with". That was our Margaret, ever popular with the guys, but fond of my children and a good *ayah* nonetheless.

One day Manaisha did not turn up for work. No message was sent giving a reason but there was nothing unusual about that. When she didn't turn up the next day either and I had to cope with my children, I went round to her house to investigate. In the street, playing with other children of her neighbourhood was a little African girl about my Mal's size wearing my Mal's dress, a dress I had made myself and was rather fond of so there was no mistake. I couldn't believe my eyes as I did believe Manaisha was honest, in spite of past warnings about all servants being thieves. On confronting Manaisha she simply shrugged her shoulders and said "Your baby has so many dresses, one less doesn't make a difference."

Of course I couldn't argue with her on this point because what she said was perfectly true. As to the ethics of it all, the meaning of Right, Wrong and taking another's belongings, any discussion on this matter would be totally wasted. She didn't see that there was an issue. This was, of course, theft, but Manaisha would never see anything wrong with a Has-Not taking from a Has-Too-Much. I just could not feel angry with Manaisha for having stolen my child's dress. I felt very guilty for having much more than my needs. I have never felt more deeply the chasm between rich and poor, the affluent world who have it all on a silver platter and the poor in the developing world whose life is a daily struggle to keep body and soul together. I had not even noticed that one of M's many dresses was missing. And I also knew she was right. My baby had a lot more than she needed whereas for her little girl it was a matter of being clothed or going naked. I remembered my Grandfather quoting a Portuguese proverb which could translate as "If you keep your coffers open even a saint will sin."

But was this action of Manaisha's a sin? Again, my Grandfather's wise words "If you leave your coffers open and someone steals, the sin is yours, not theirs". It was up to me not to put temptation in her path. I heeded my mother-in-law's advice to "take it for granted all servants are thieves and you can never prove otherwise – keep everything under lock and key". So I kept my jewellery and valuables locked up. But how can you lock up all your clothes and pots and pans and children's toys? I didn't appreciate then the blessing of not having to lock up the children. Children were safe there. Nobody would kidnap them and nobody would harm them. These are dangers of the Western, so-called 'civilised', world. People in Tanzania loved children. I don't remember ever having heard the terms NAI (non-accidental injury), child battering or sex abuse.

Many were the moral dilemmas which faced me in Tanzania. Is theft simply taking something that does not belong to you? Is the taking of a loaf of bread by a starving man as sinful as the swindling of money that people in high positions or in business did all the time? What about giving a job to your nephew when a man with a family to feed might be more competent? Is that moral?

Yes, Tanzania taught me a lot and provided food for thought in abundance. I do believe I became more tolerant in my attitude to many things in life – philosophical questions, moral dilemmas. Is there absolute Right and Wrong? Truth and Lies? Honesty and Dishonesty? The list is long. But questioning did broaden my mind... I hope.

Ayah Lucia (1959)

Ayah Manaisha with baby Reethah (1961)

Sindano

Sindano means needle. Needle means injection. A *sindano* was the cure of all ills in East Africa and the sine qua non of all cures. It mattered little what a patient complained of. It mattered not what the doctor thought was the best treatment for that ailment. They had to give a *sindano*. Without it, no patient felt cured. Without it, a patient felt cheated. Without it, no doctor got paid for his services. A doctor who gave no sindano didn't know their job. And this applied to all communities and ethnic groups.

I soon found out that, in this part of the world, the curing of patients simply by laying one's hands on them was not deemed a miracle. At first, in my case, however, it seemed that no patient could be cured with using hands, pills or even potions. Healing is more than curing a medical ailment with a diagnosis; healing is psychological and if an infection is treated or worms are expelled or a rash disappears, a person is not healed if in their mind they don't believe themselves to be healed.

So, in short: no *sindano*, no cure! As a corollary, no *sindano* also meant no fee because however real the success in the doctor's eyes, it was still a failure in the patient's. So the choice was, if a patient needed penicillin they had a *sindano* as opposed to the oral form. If they needed a drug that didn't come in the form of an injection, they were given the correct pill or potion… then an injection anyway.

When we arrived in Tanga the other doctors were well seasoned and knew the ropes. I suppose they had had their turn at learning the hard way as I did. The first patient I treated with medicine in tablet form looked at me with disdain and said "What! No *sindano*? I want a *sindano*!" The next simply refused to pay my fee because I had not 'really' treated her although she felt better with the tablets. Soon I knew with a heavy heart – and a heavier conscience – that I was standing on a crossroads. Many was the sleepless night of internal turmoil. Should I stick to my principles or should I slacken them and do the practical and sensible thing for survival? My internal debate between reason and conscience went on and on.

Watu

Watu is Kiswahili for "people". It still amazes me how the innumerable communities in East Africa lived together in harmony. Communities of people from different backgrounds, origins, cultures, religions. I cannot say they had a close relationship as equals, but everyone knew their place and seemed to be comfortable in their particular niche. They never intermarried but were good friends. They didn't even invite one another to their homes but took gifts of food to members of other communities on their own feast days. Where do I start? Let me begin at home.

My new family were Gujarati, Brahman, Hindu. Gujarati Hindus were the largest group after native Africans. But you could not lump them together either. There were Brahmans, Banias, Loanas, Patels and other castes. These again, did not intermarry. The majority of Hindus were merchants of one sort or another. Trade was so deeply ingrained in them that it and money affected and ruled their views, values and attitudes to everything in life; as I have already touched upon, this is something I found quite abhorrent and shocking from the start.

The Indians first went to East Africa at the end of

the 19thcentury as indentured labourers to build the Mombasa-Uganda Railway. They were poor but hard-working and hoped to improve their lot. At first there were only men. Those with families left them behind in India. Later they took their families, and bachelors returned to India to find wives. Later, in the early 20th century, another band of immigrants, mostly merchants, went and settled in East Africa As time went by they started running businesses and very successfully too. They had shops, mostly in towns, but some went into distant villages, miles from 'civilisation'. At the time when my husband was growing up in the 1940s and 1950s many families sent their sons to study in India or a few in England. That was how I met my husband in India at Medical School. We had so many students from East Africa.

The other Indians in East Africa were various sects of Muslims: the Bohras, Sunni, mostly merchants; the Ismailis, Shia, in all kinds of businesses, quite westernised; the Ishnashris whose women wore the burkha… There was a good number of Punjabis, Sindhis, Sikhs, South Indians and Goans. Many in clerical jobs. Africans, of course, were the local people and in numbers were the majority. In the social hierarchy, however, they fell at the lower end. Some had small shops in African areas. The better off had *shambas* (small holdings) outside town and others did jobs of all kinds including domestic service. Prejudice against Africans by Indians was always pervasive.

The easy relationships between African men and women were always a source of wonder and amusement to me. I never saw a marriage so assumed that a man and a woman just lived together for as long as they both so wished. If not, they parted. Each one then might find another partner. And any children born while a couple were together went with mother when the parents parted. Father never had to be taken to court for support of his children. He always continued to financially and otherwise support his own children.

Our servants were always African; some excellent, some quite awful (a range reflecting the rest of humanity). I don't quite remember what an African family was like. Most were Muslim, some Christian and some (I can only assume) had no religion. Muslim men had more than one wife if they could afford it. The better off would have one wife and her children in town looking after a shop and another with her children in the village looking after a *shamba*. African names often amused me. Many had Christian names which they pronounced with an "i" at the end: Pauli, Davidi, Tomasi. Those with Christian names might be Muslim, or the other way round, or be of no particular religion. The Swahili names I found particularly amusing. A man came into the surgery.

"What is your name", I asked.

"*Mimi Simba bin Funda*", he replied. "I am Lion son of Donkey."

Another man brought his new baby daughter and proudly presented her, proclaiming:

"my new baby, her name is Headneck."

The Arabs in East Africa lived along the coast of Tanganyika (later Tanzania), Zanzibar and Kenya. They came by *dhow* (ships with large triangular sails and one or two masts) from the Arabian peninsula, mainly from the Yemen and they were traders. They were the most wonderful patients I ever had and many of my most memorable experiences are to do with them. They had *dukas* in town and out in the bush. Their family units were very large comprising all the brothers and their wives and children, their old parents and other relatives. The normal set-up was a little shop in front through which you had to go to reach their living quarters at the back. At the back there was always an *oani*, an open space which served many purposes: washing clothes and vessels, gossiping, a safe playground for the children. I always thought their children grew up in a very loving, safe and caring environment.

Wazungu (Europeans, singular *Mzungu*) did not mix with any others except in unavoidable transactions such as giving orders to servants at home or barmen at the club, or staff at the office.

They had all the top jobs before Independence. They were mainly British with some Italians, Greeks and Eastern Europeans. The British were the bosses in offices. Other Europeans were usually entrepreneurs who did extremely well before finally going home with full pockets.

The British never bothered to learn the local language, Kiswahili. Instead, the local Africans, most of whom could not read, write or sign their names, learnt English. There was a terribly colonial attitude of arrogance and superiority on the part of the British.

* * *

Khojas (also known as Ismailis) are a sect of Shia Muslims. Their spiritual leader has the title of Aga Khan. He was a very wealthy and influential man and lived in Canada. The Khoja community was one I greatly admired. There was a large community in Tanga with very well organised services for their people in the fields of education, health and social services. No member was ever stark poor, hungry or homeless. They had financial help for the poor, the needy, widows and orphans. They had well run schools and there was no illiteracy among them. Their men wore European clothes and the women, particularly the young, wore European style dresses while the older ones preferred long gowns with a scarf to cover the head. They had large and close-knit families as a rule.

There was a large Mosque in Tanga where not only were their religious services carried out but which also served in other areas such as administrative offices for the various services they offered to their members. Here they also ran a clinic in another part of the complex; there was a daily clinic run by Dr T for men and families and a twice-weekly clinic for women and children which I attended to for several years. The clinic was well run and organised and well equipped.

On Fridays you could see them all making their way to the Mosque, carrying a covered dish. I was told these were cooked items of food which were sold after the service and the proceeds went to the Mosque. Thus people contributed to funds and others who couldn't or didn't feel like cooking had a ready meal. What an excellent idea!

They also had their own private schools where the standard of teaching was high. Outsiders were not barred but paid full fees. Ismailis attended free or had fees subsidised, based on their means. I always enjoyed my sessions at the Mosque and had a good relationship with the leaders and managers and patients. They treated the doctors well with respect as professionals, not as merchants like my husband's community did. The Ismaili community took pride in promoting good health in their members and we immunised children and had well-women sessions among other things. Looking back on it now, it was all quite forward-thinking.

Once a year they organised a health contest for children in various age groups with prizes and, most admirably, there was a contest for women of various age groups so even very elderly ladies could take part. I have not heard of any such contest for older women anywhere else. They invited professional women from Dar es Salaam and Mombasa as judges and at the presentation of prizes always acknowledged my services to the community, thanked me and gave me a lovely gift. I felt respected and treasured by this community as I respected and treasured them in return.

Once we had a visit from their spiritual leader, the Aga Khan and I had the privilege of shaking his hand. He lived in Canada but cared for all his followers all over the world. His father had once married the actress Rita Hayworth, and his grandfather, a man of immense physique, had been weighed-in against diamonds at his diamond jubilee, after which I expect all the associated wealth was distributed to the community. When the political situation became difficult in Tanzania and a lot of Asians of all denominations, including my family, left hoping for a better, albeit unknown, future in other lands, the Aga Khan helped his people, and many Ismailis from Tanga emigrated to Canada where he helped them to find jobs, housing and generally settle down.

Ismaili mosque

Mahila Mandal

In India a *mahila mandal* is a social club which helps women with education, health advice and those sorts of things. There was a regular women's group in Tanga which was known as *Mahila Mandal.* Upon hearing of it I, of course, assumed they did the same. I had heard of many other women's groups and associations all over the world and of their activities.

I assumed at *Mahila Mandal* they taught themselves arts and crafts.
I assumed they had activities to improve themselves.
I assumed they did charitable works and raised funds for charity.
I assumed... ass-u-me'd... Ass U Me!
When I assume, I make an ass out of 'u' and 'me'.

I was invited to join the Club, so I went to the next meeting. I was not late but the room was already crowded. About 20 women of assorted ages, sizes and shapes were squatted, squeezed onto a rush mat. Twenty pairs of eyes looked at me and followed my every move. They sounded welcoming, with "*ah-oh, ah-oh!*" ("come, come", the equivalent of "welcome" in Gujarati). They squeezed some more and made place for me. Without hesitation I sat on the floor as well and tried to chat with the women near me. I soon realised that the meeting was literally just that… meeting and gossiping. The *Mahila Mandal* did nothing else.

I come from a family where everyone is highly educated, both boys and girls. Whatever other people of my society may or may not have believed, since an early age I have believed in equality, whatever the caste, sex, finances or fame. One may be richer, cleverer, wiser, socially of a higher status than another, but no human is better than the next. I was privileged to have been born into a family that lived to very high standards in every way, but had also been taught about the responsibilities that go with that privilege. This lesson had not been in words but example. So I had no problem sitting on the floor with the uneducated women of the town.

But I was naïve enough to imagine I would teach them something and improve their lot. I discovered the hard way that being unassuming only had the opposite effect. In this community (to which I was now tied down by marriage), it was arrogance, superiority complexes and showing off that got you respect.

What a come-down – a crash-down!

I duly squatted on the rush mat. There was pin-drop silence and they all just stared at me. Women? Silent? Very unusual. It was getting rather tense and I was beginning to regret having come. Finally, a woman coughed and the spell was broken and suddenly it was all jabber, jabber again.

"Meenakshi is going to Lusaka to have her baby there and to be with her family. The hospitals there are very good, not like the rubbish here."

"My neighbour Hassan is closing shop and moving somewhere else. His business is not doing well." "What do you expect? He cheats and never gives you the right weight of your goods."

There was no end of information freely and loudly available about all and sundry. I didn't hear a single thing educational or constructive mentioned. No talk of charity, but rather total lack of it in the gossip about everyone in town. I had to shift my position several times and still was getting cramp squatting on the mat, which I was not at all used to.

"Umaben, I have this pain in my back. I can't sleep at night. What shall I do?"

"Umaben, my periods are very irregular, what can you do for me?"

"Umaben, my baby gets a lot of colic. What is it due to?"

Soon this was turning into a free clinic and it was useless advising women in public, without detailed information or examination and in the presence of all those eyes and ears. After an hour I could not take it any more and abruptly said "I have to go now, time to attend my surgery". I could hardly stand up with the cramp in my legs. I practically hobbled to the door, with 20 pairs of eyes following every painful step until I disappeared through the door.

Some days later I was asked to give a talk to the group with topic left to my discretion. "What would be of interest to these women?" I wondered. In the end I decided on health care during pregnancy, labour and post-partum. I had faith in my subject but my Gujarati was not up to scratch. I could manage to converse, but giving a talk is another matter. I had no help of slides or anything else. The lack of aids and my poor mastery of the language made this project quite daunting. But I had agreed to it and did my best. It was bad enough using ordinary words but medical words I could not cope with and had to say them in English. I talked about diet and specific exercises during pregnancy, a subject I passionately believed in, but was aware these women would never do them. I told them about the stages of labour and what happens to a woman's body during pregnancy, labour and after as I know a lot of women are so frightened because they don't know what is happening to them.

Somehow I got through my talk, then asked them if they had any questions. All the questions had to do with food, things such as what is good and what is bad for women when they are pre- and post natal.

"Is it okay to have yoghurt when you have just had a baby?"

"Is it okay to have hot, spicy food when you have just had a baby?"

I did not immediately realise these were trick questions to put me to the test. Their retorts to my replies were many.

"Everybody knows it is bad to have yoghurt, it gives one infection."

"Everyone knows it is bad to have spicy food because it causes bleeding."

I wanted some feedback on how my talk had come across but I couldn't directly ask. As it happened, I didn't need to try. It soon came to my ears that the women thought this nurse who calls herself a doctor doesn't know simple things that everybody knows. She recommends yoghurt even to a recently delivered woman and she advises exercises during pregnancy. Everyone knows that can cause a miscarriage.

I sadly realised I could never educate these women – women who did not want to be educated for they 'knew it all already' and whose prejudices would always win. The women (and I take it the men as well) were uneducated but certainly not humble. What they knew or believed had been handed down from generation to generation through the ages, from small villages in India. Was there a chance of educating them? No way. If you told them anything different from what they believed, it was you who were stupid, even if the subject was health and you were a qualified doctor.

These people believed that every illness is either 'hot or 'cold', that is if it is something that causes fever, it is hot. If you have a cold or sneeze, it is cold. Every food item, similarly, is either 'heating' (like a hot, spicy curry) or 'cooling' (cold drinks, yoghurts) and for a hot illness you give cooling food, and heating food for a cold illness. Simple enough? Simplistic? Definitely. They believed one must not give a cold drink to someone suffering from a 'cold' illness. When I told the women that, contrary to their belief, it's okay to give yoghurt to a woman who has recently given birth, they did not learn something they did not know. They thought "She doesn't even know it is bad to give yoghurt to a woman in such circumstances. And she calls herself a Doctor!" I could not win at any level with the women of my husband's community.

When I poured out my disappointment to a Colleague in Dar, she comforted me. "Don't you realise it is pure jealousy? These women's lives revolve around cooking and child-rearing. They have no importance in their male-dominated society, no excitement in their lives. Putting you down is the most exciting thing that has ever happened to them. You just have to rise above it all, not let them pull you down to their level." I believe she was right.

I tried to act superior but it was against the grain and it was too late. This experience taught me one of the greatest lessons in Life: 'be yourself'. You are then at peace with yourself and it doesn't matter if the whole world is against you.

That was the end of my Mahila Mandal.

Reethah's Birth

In 1960 I was expecting my second baby. My workload did not abate. Neither did my cough. Tanga Province had large sisal estates and produced one-fifth of the world's sisal, the fibre used for rope, mats and such things. The atmosphere was charged with microscopic particles of sisal which caused havoc with people's chests. I suffered with severe asthma during my time in Tanga and coughed almost continuously for the nine years we were there until I ended up with a prolapse of the womb. I felt much relief when we went to the seaside on Sunday evenings, but Ashok refused to rent a house in Raskazone, the seaside area; he wouldn't agree to the expense, even though we earned so much and could well afford it.

If I wasn't in the surgery at nine sharp, Ashok would phone home. "What are you doing? There is a queue of women waiting here". Rush to nursery to drop Mal, then rush to surgery. When a fit of cough came in the middle of examining a patient, I had to stop, go to the next room and cough it out. Late in the morning, if there were a few minutes between patients, I would sit down and put a few stitches into a tapestry I was doing, and which depicted a man in a brown hat sitting by a stream, fishing. I enjoyed putting in every stitch in that tapestry but managed to finish it only when my secondborn Reethah was two years old. I still have it in my Guest-Room.

One evening Ashok came home and announced to me that a couple had asked for an abortion and, without my consent or consultation, had agreed that I would do it. He had arranged and collected the fee and when they should come next morning. I had never done an abortion in my life and never intended to do one as (in those days) it went against my beliefs; besides, it was illegal too. He had come to me with a fait accompli. That night I didn't sleep a wink. I most definitely did not want to do it but would have to face Ashok's wrath in the morning when I told him so. I have done many things in my life, like signing off my house to his sister, as a result of the fear of my husband's wrath which never failed to intimidate but I couldn't do this deed. I would need all my courage and more to face him. All night I tossed and turned and had visions of something terrible happening to my baby if I agreed. I believe it was the thought of my unborn baby that gave me the courage to face up to him in the morning and refuse. I was proud of myself when I stood up to him and faced the tune for the first time in my life. How he faced the tune with the patient's husband I daren't think.

* * *

Safira came regularly to see me with one complaint or another. She was expecting again. Her previous delivery had been a tragedy. I had looked after her during pregnancy and had been asked to do her delivery. The delivery was very quick, being her third. One big push and the baby was out. To my utter horror, the umbilical cord, which was exceptionally long, had wound itself round the baby's neck three times and as the baby was pushed out, it strangled it. Baby came out purple and limp and never took its first breath. There was nothing I could have done about it and they could have easily blamed me for the tragedy but they didn't. I was so grateful and admiring of the attitude of the family. They were aware it was not my fault and put it down to Allah's will and no more was said about it. They continued to come to me with their medical problems.

After her previous experience, one would have thought she would never want to see me again. Far from it. Her unwavering faith in me was very touching and I felt the weight of responsibility. She was at the same stage of pregnancy as myself. When we were seven months pregnant her husband came to see me and asked me to do her delivery. I said "I'm sorry, but I am due at around the same time and will be going to Dar es Salaam for my own delivery". "No, no, you <u>must</u> do it. She will wait for you", he said with such conviction.

The hospital in Tanga, like many others, had such a terrible reputation. Patients refused to be sent there, holding the prevailing attitude that "you only go there to die". A colleague had said "I wouldn't send my dog there". I certainly did not want to send myself there to have my baby. I couldn't have my baby at home either so we had decided I would go to Dar es Salaam for my delivery where Ashok's sister Sushila lived and we could stay a few days with her before and after. In retrospect I'm appalled to think I didn't make any contingency plans in case I went into early labour.

A week before I was due, we left Mal with Motiben (Ashok's eldest sister) and I flew to Dar es Salaam to my sister-in-law Sushila's. My old colleague from medical school, Meera, had her own nursing home in Dar es Salaam and it was arranged I would have my baby there. My relations with Sushila had never been cordial. On the surface she was always good to me but I always got the feeling it was not because she cared for me but to show the world she treated me well. That was the ethic in their family, "So we can say X", "so they can't say Y". Meera was 2 years senior to me at medical school. She was a Maharashtrian Hindu and had married for love a colleague who was a Ismaili Muslim. They have had a very happy marriage which is still successful after 45 years. Meera's nursing home was small but well run and efficient like her. She treated me extremely well and was not only my doctor, but a mother to me, something I desperately needed.

Baby Reethah arrived on cue at a bouncy 8lb 10oz. She gave no trouble at all, there was no complication at delivery and the week I spent at the nursing home was bliss for me, except for missing my Mal of course. She had been looking forward to the arrival of a new baby and would hug and kiss my tummy and pray in her toddler fashion, in Gujarati "*Bapa*, please give me a nice *toto*" (baby or child in Kiswahili). My new baby was perfect and a joy to behold and cuddle.

It was strange (or at least it was at the time) that I didn't miss Ashok and he didn't come to visit me or take me home. It was much later that I learnt that Meera had thought his absence strange. Ashok of course didn't want to lose income, which he would have done by coming to Dar for a day. Another nail in the coffin of my marriage.

Reethah was a gorgeous baby, so peaceful and undemanding, never giving me a sleepless night, only pure joy. She kept my spirits up at a time when they were sagging badly. Breastfeeding too was no problem. On the seventh day I flew home with the new baby. Ashok took us home from the airport. Little Mal was over the moon and bounced up and down right at the airport. Then we went home. Surprise, Surprise! What did I have waiting for me and a new baby? A nice cup of tea? Putting my feet up? A lovely bunch of flowers? No such luck. Not even a glass of water! There were two patients waiting to be seen by me right in my home. He had told them the time I was due back and asked them to come to the house as I couldn't go to the surgery. How could I let down my faithful patients who showed such loyalty? Obviously my husband had less qualms about letting his wife down.

The next day Safira's husband came to call. She had gone into labour. As good as her promise she had waited for me. I said "but, Mbarak, I have just come out of hospital, my baby is only a week old". "You don't have to do anything, Mama, just be there. The women in the house will do everything". I fed my baby and rushed to Safira. This time it all went well and quick. I returned home in time for my own baby's next feed. I plucked up courage to put my foot down and tell Ashok that I wanted some days off to recuperate and I didn't want to see patients but wanted to enjoy being at home and being a mum. The next day I stayed at home thoroughly enjoying my babies.

Some time in the day I went to the patio outside the front door of the flat to hang some clothes on the line. Toddler Mal was fiddling with the door and managed to latch the door from inside and lock herself and baby in. There was no way I could get inside. I panicked She wanted to come out to me but couldn't so got very agitated. "Open the door, Mummy!" she screamed and as I couldn't she got more and more agitated. "Open the door. Open the door. Why don't you open the door", she screamed. "If you don't open I'm going to beat the baby." By now I was even more agitated than the toddler. I was out of my wits and couldn't think how I could get in.

Finally I rushed to my next door neighbour Maniben for help. Thank goodness her teenage son Bipin was in. Our balconies were adjoining and there was a narrow ledge between them. Luckily again my balcony door into the living room was open. Bipin climbed out of his balcony, on to the ledge and on to my balcony and so into my house and managed to open my door to the patio. Thank God for teenagers! How I hugged my babies! Most lessons in life we learn from mistakes and mishaps; some turn out to be very expensive. I learnt not to leave toddlers alone with door latches; the experience left me with that nugget of wisdom. We learn so little of our total wisdom from the books we read.

My cough and wheezing returned and I had to take tablets. At the time only tablets with ephedrine were available for asthma. My milk dried up very quickly. I had hardly managed to breastfeed my baby for a month. Fortunately Reethah thrived on Cow and Gate. The representative for Cow and Gate offered me limitless supplies in return for keeping a chart of baby's weight and general progress. Later, when she was weaned I was also given supplies of baby cereal.

The family in Raskazone (1963)

Baby Reethah aged 7 months (1962)

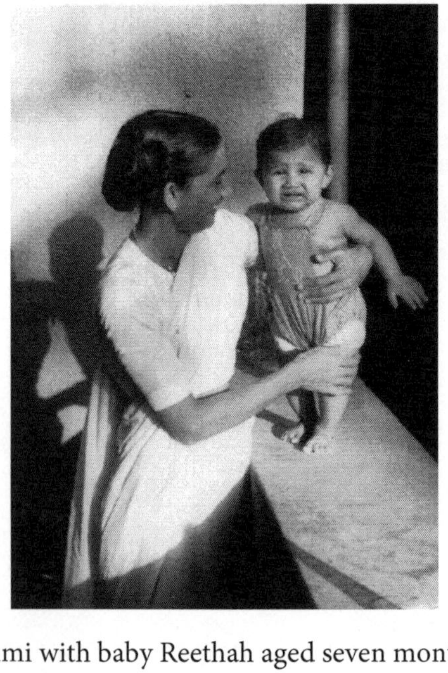

Mimi with baby Reethah aged seven months (1962)

Milk, Veg, Fish

One of the many things that were so different from England in our time in Tanga, and which I remember with great nostalgia, was the personal supply of food to the door by the milkman, the vegetable man (whom *ayah* Margaret would always flirt with) and the fishmonger. The *tring-tring* of the milkman's bike was a very cheerful and welcome sound. He carried two large canisters of milk, one on either side of the back wheel, and a measuring can with a long handle. Milk was not pasteurised so had to be boiled as soon as it was bought, cooled and put in the fridge. It was not standardised either and many a milkman watered it down to go further. Then housewives started to arm themselves with hydrometers to test the specific density of the milk. I have forgotten now what it should be, but we could tell if it was thinned down.

Of course then the milkmen got wise to this in their turn, and added some flour to the watered down milk. Fortunately for us our faithful hydrometer could still tell the difference. I decided the best thing was to come out in the open and had a chat with my milkman. He would sell me unadulterated milk and I would stick to him for my supply and give the custom of my mother-in-law, sister-in-law and friends. Or he could continue to adulterate the milk and lose my custom. It worked. It made an honest man of the milkman but I must confess that now and again I did check the milk with the hydrometer but always after he had gone. He kept his promise and never betrayed my trust.

Then there was the vegetable man. He came with a box on wheels which he pushed along. The smell of fresh vegetables and fruit was tantalising – aubergines, gourds, okra, breadfruit, cassava and others besides the humdrum potatoes and onions. He also sold fruit – bananas, papayas, guavas, apples, starfruit. When I first came to England I detested bananas as they were such a far cry from the naturally sun-ripened fruit of East Africa. The range of banana types available was quite amazing, from the small, fat *membu* variety bursting out of their thin skins and which simply melt in the mouth (a big hit with my baby Mal when she was weaned), through various sizes and colours to the cooking variety known as *matoki* which is the staple food in Uganda.

The wares of the fish-man were also a joy. Not only was the fish always fresh but there was such a variety of it. Our favourite was mackerel (about half the size of the Cornish variety) and pomfret, both excellent for frying plain or stuffed with Indian spices. Top of my list was prawns. In England we buy some 100 to 250g at a time and they are frozen and quite tasteless and so expensive. We used to buy a kilo or two at a time; large, juicy, king prawns and the recipes for prawns were endless – curry, masala-fry, prawn-pie and so on and so forth. My mouth is watering as I write this.

The food in East Africa was always fresh and organic. I didn't even know the word “organic” then and took it for granted that all food was healthy. We didn’t have processed foods either and I can't help comparing the food in England with what we had back there. When we first came to England I used to eat apples unpared until someone said I shouldn't because of pesticides and wax covering. Some time later somebody else said “don’t you eat the skin? It is the most nutritious part of the fruit”. I still don't know which option is better. I believe we ate a much healthier diet in Tanzania. In England people not only overeat and suffer with obesity, but food is riddled with additives and other unhealthy constituents. Obviously a financially wealthier country is not necessarily a healthier one.

Mimi's tapestry as it now hangs in her house
(2014)

More Patients

I was called to see 12 year old Asha Mehta. She had been running a temperature and complained of abdominal pain. I arrived at the house and was taken straight in. I set down my case and pulled out my stethoscope. I had not had the chance to even take the patient's pulse or touch her when the father barged in. "It's okay, you can go now; our usual Doctor has arrived." Without as much as an apology I was dismissed.

If I stayed a minute longer I would be confronting a colleague in a patient's room and we would both be facing a most embarrassing encounter. To avoid this situation I quickly put my things back in the case and left, bumping into Dr K on the way out. We wished each other and I walked on to my car. At the gate I bumped into Dr S who had also been called. I dreaded to think of the embarrassment he would be facing on entering this house. So I mentioned the position to him. I don't know how he handled it because I couldn't wait to get into my car to drive off. Had I been a plumber or electrician in England I would have been entitled to charge and demand a call-out fee. Being a doctor in Tanga legally and technically I could have charged a fee and if all the three doctors decided to do the same Mr Mehta would have had to pay for three visits. but we would never have got our money but for going to court and it wasn't worth the agro.

Young Deepa Shah was suffering from malaria. Her temperature was 104˚F. She was critically ill as not only was she having an acute bout of malaria but she had had it before, was very anaemic and had persistent vomiting. I visited and treated her. The next day I visited again to follow-up.

"How is she?", I asked.

"No better", the mother said sullenly.

I took the girl's temperature; it was 100ºF. She was no longer vomiting and could hold down fluids.

"Is her temperature lower than yesterday?" I asked.

"Yes", mother said reluctantly.

"Is the vomiting better?"

"Yes", was the barely audible reply.

"Would you not say she is better, then?"

"But she still has fever", mother said ungratefully.

In this community there was no winning. If patients got cured it was never appreciated. If they didn't, the consequence was 'character murder'.

How often I had to remind myself to "not let the Hate go to your heart!"

Baby Kapadia was brought to the surgery with

diarrhoea, patient advised and treatment given. Off went mother and baby. The next day I was invited to a religious ceremony at the house of a Mr Ashok Patel. As usual, after religion came food and gossip. Suddenly I hear loudly from across the room, loud enough for all to hear, "Umaben, your medicine is useless, my baby is still not alright". In this case I had the presence of mind to shout back loudly enough for all to hear my reply as well (she was on the other side of the room), "In that case you'd better find yourself another doctor and don't ever come back to me". I could hardly believe I had said that. What was happening to me?

Houseboy

All the Europeans and Indians in East Africa had a houseboy (except my in-laws), an adult or young man. He did all the housework, cleaned the house, washed clothes by hand (no washing machines in those days), ironed, cooked or helped with food preparation, did shopping, helped carry the *mehmsab's* (lady of the house) shopping… the list was endless! A jack of all trades called, in a nutshell, a houseboy.

When I arrived in Tanzania, one of the first pieces of advice I was given by practically everybody was that Africans are all thieves and you can't prove otherwise. They can't and shouldn't be trusted. In law it is said a man is innocent until proved otherwise. Regarding African servants it was a question of "They are all thieves and you can't prove otherwise". I have already mentioned uncle's servant in Jinja who faithfully worked for them until he died of old age and never stole a thing. I desperately wanted to prove the belief wrong and trusted my servants but sadly was proved wrong myself on several occasions.

There was Ramadhani, about 25 years old. He was good at his work. He cooked and cleaned and was efficient. I once gave him money to buy a dozen eggs. He returned saying he had fallen from his bike and all the eggs had broken. I could not believe that not even one had been spared and took him in my car to show me the spot where he had fallen. There should have been a big mess on the road but there was nothing. We discharged him.

Then there was Husseini, again very good at his work. I regret that due to my trusting nature I often opened a locked drawer where I kept money within his view, to give him money for shopping. We always locked our bedroom door when we went out. One day we came home to find he had broken the door lock, got into the bedroom and broken into the money drawer. It had all been well planned well in advance. The drawer was empty and much else was gone, as was Husseini. We did manage to catch him and report him to the Police. I attended his trial. He was charged and sent to prison. I went to the prison to visit him and took him food.

Unbelievably, when he came out of prison, I gave him another chance. And guess what? He continued pilfering again and was discharged. A couple of years later we found he was working for an elderly Indian man living alone in the *shamba* and had been robbing him right, left and centre but he had managed to gain trust from the old man and sadly, due to his old age, managed to fleece him without suspicion.

But every rule has exceptions. In the last few years of our life in Tanga we employed Maulidi Rashidi; what a treasure he turned out to be. Maulidi had a wife and six children. He had a Muslim name but was a Catholic. He had a very small *shamba* in the country, far from enough to provide for his large family, so the wife and older children looked after the *shamba* whilst Maulidi took up employment in town as a houseboy for which he got a very modest but regular income. It was our good fortune that he took up employment with us.

Maulidi was a marvel, a real Mr Belvedere. He excelled at everything he did. He cooked, cleaned, washed the floor and the cars, he changed bulbs and punctured tyres, he washed and ironed. In fact, it seemed there was nothing he could not do. The first part of Maulidi's daily routine was: make breakfast before we left home in the morning; sweep and mop the bungalow; wash by hand all the clothes of 5 family members; put them out to dry out in the blazing sun; cook lunch and something for dinner (he remembered what each of my children liked and cooked accordingly). After our lunch, Maulidi went up to the terrace to have his. His lunch consisted of some of our food, but mainly *ugali*, the local staple made from white cornmeal and similar to polenta. Just as I did all those years before in Goa in my childhood with our *ayah*, my children went up to the terrace and ate *ugali* from Maulidi's plate. They have fond memories of this, as I have of eating off my *ayah's* plate.

Now, Maulidi would wash up, then dry and iron all the clothes – such a big pile! It was so hot that we needed to change all our clothes, including night clothes every day, and we were a family of five! After that he even swept and mopped the house again. In that climate there is so much dust, at 5.00pm you wouldn't guess the house had been dusted that morning.

If a bulb needed changing, "Maulidi! Maulidi!"

If a tyre needed changing, "Maulidi! Maulidi!"

Each year Maulidi went home to his family in the country for ten days. The next year there was a new baby. By the time we left, Maulidi had nine children. That year I had a talk with him and advised him on contraception. I should have done this much earlier and regret I didn't. The last time he was going home I took him to the railway station. I wanted to give him some contraceptive to take home. I was late returning home from work and had to rush for him to catch the train. On the way I stopped at a chemist. I happened to park the car in front of the shop and in full view of the chemist himself. I always made Maulidi sit on the front passenger seat when I had to take him anywhere. I rushed in, in a great hurry, and huffing and puffing asked the chemist for condoms. He looked out of the shop and there right in front saw a black man sitting in the seat right next to mine and me huffing and puffing, asking for condoms. Did he raise an eyebrow! No, <u>both</u>!

One of the great regrets of my life is that we totally lost contact with Maulidi when we left. In East Africa post is not delivered at home but you need a post box for which you have to pay. Poor people can't afford one and Maulidi certainly did not have one. He gave me his son's employer's post box, but I reckon his son must have left the job because I never got a reply when I wrote from England. And so we totally lost touch with our Maulidi. It saddened me so much that I couldn't send him money. £5 a month was no pinch for me but it would have greatly helped this remarkable man, his wife and nine children.

Maulidi in front of the
Dar es Salaam bungalow (1970)

Murderess

Murat Ali was an orthodox Ishnashri Muslim, a community whose womenfolk wore the *burqa*. The family regularly came to me with their medical problems. In the early hours of a Thursday, Murat Ali came to call me to see his daughter Razia. She was 19 and expecting her first baby. She was already anaemic and a rather weakly girl. I did not like what I saw. She had had small bouts of bleeding every now and then but the family had not felt concerned enough to inform me. Now she had another and bigger bout and looked poorly so the parents worried. I diagnosed placenta praevia and in view of her condition and the history and in spite of the experience with Somabhai's daughter and the risk of losing another family, I advised them to take the girl to hospital. "Hospital?! People only go there to die. I'm not having her in hospital. Doctor, you do what she needs right here at home".

"But there is not much I can do and the girl is in danger", I tried to persuade them. He almost fell at my feet with hands together and begged "You just do what you can, but please don't send her to hospital. My mother died there and whatever happens, we don't want Razia to go". The father was adamant. "But I can't take the responsibility. These cases can suddenly get much worse and it can be dangerous." "We won't hold you responsible. Do what you can, but do it at home." "Alright, in that case I'll keep an eye on her, but if her condition worsens, I cannot take responsibility and you will have no alternative."

I was so concerned I could not leave the girl that night. Having worked all day as usual and done my family duties, I left my 2 little girls with my husband and spent all night in the patient's house, trying to catch some sleep on an easy chair on the veranda and putting up with the heat and the mosquitoes. Of course I had no sleep at all. The night was uneventful and in the morning I returned to my home, family and surgery. On Friday night I slept, (or tried to) in Murat Ali's house again on the easy chair. Not a wink of sleep again. In the early hours Razia had another bout of bleeding and I felt both her condition and the baby's were serious and I could no longer take responsibility. I had to put my foot down.

The family gathered and we discussed. I stressed yet again how urgent and serious the situation was. "We'll have to think about it" said Murat Ali. He sent for his 2 brothers who had shops in outlying villages and his aunt who was with her daughter in another. They all came and conferred and decided to heed my advice. Razia was taken by car to the hospital. The family believed in Allah's wish and that day I believed in Fate.

Being a Saturday the hospital was even worse staffed than usual. All the European doctors went off for the weekend by the afternoon. The remaining staff decided to do a caesarean when the consultant returned on Monday morning. But Allah's wish was to take Razia on Sunday. To this day I don't know whether the outcome might have been different if I had been more insistent she go to the hospital on that first day, or the family had heeded my advice. But now it was too late. A 19 year-old girl expecting her first baby was dead. Yet, the family did not blame me.

The next day I heard rumours that people in the town were practically shouting "Mrs D killed Murat Ali's daughter". It must have been true because three families who had pregnant daughters in my care came to the surgery very sullen and disdainful and cancelled their request for my care. It was a terrible crush. Was it worth caring for these narrow-minded people? Could I really do any good for the Gujaratis of Tanga? What had I sacrificed my sleep, time with my own babies, my own health and my leisure for? Was it all to any good? I visited Razia's family to offer them comfort in their loss and was a little comforted myself when Murat Ali took my hand and covered it with his tears and said from his heart "We know you did your best and you warned us. It was Allah's will."

Dudu

Dudu in Swahili is a general name that encompasses many creatures from germs, insects, creepy-crawlies to worms. All these we had plenty of in Tanzania. There were roundworms, threadworms, tapeworms, bilharzia, mango-fly and many, many more. Out of the long list, I'm glad to say, my family were not affected by any of the worms. But the mango-fly I have mentioned I shall never forget.

The most common of all were malaria-carrying mosquitoes. Malaria affects half the world's population and is a deadly disease causing over 500,000 fatalities per year. One develops partial immunity to malaria. I suffered with bouts of malaria for a few years and will never forget the suffering: very high fever with severe shivering, terrible aches all over leaving one utterly exhausted. It also leads to anaemia. Surprisingly neither Ashok nor any of the children ever got it.

Ants were everywhere. You couldn't leave sugar or anything sweet on a table without a trail of ants marching towards it within minutes. We had to store sugar in a pot on an "island", a stand surrounded by water. There was a large variety of ants in the house and outside. I have already mentioned the variety *siafu*. Cockroaches were also a plague. However clean your house, they would colonise especially the kitchen in no time. Every kitchen had cockroach powder sprinkled all around the floor edge.

There are over 300 parasites that the human species has inherited from our primate ancestors. Roundworms: practically every African child had roundworms. These worms use the human body to stay alive, feed and reproduce. One gets the infestation from contaminated food and water. When the infestation was mild or even moderate there were no signs, but often it was severe. Then the child would be thin and pale with a pot-belly. The abdominal wall was so thin one could actually see a mass of worms wriggling inside. Fortunately the treatment was simple. I was once called to see a child who, while doing a poo out on the ground, had a worm half in and half out and it wasn't shifting a long time. A dose of castor oil solved the problem.

Guinea-worm infestation is a very ancient disease. It is described in the Bible as well as being shown in Egyptian papyri of 1500BCE and found in mummies. It is caused by the females of the largest nematode (a class of worms) infesting humans. When they are ready to release eggs, they perforate the skin on the leg and start pushing out. The treatment was to wind the worm as it emerges, round a matchstick, a few inches every day. The Rod of Asclepius, symbol of Medicine, is thought to have been inspired by this stick.

Bilharzia infestation (also known as schistosomiasis) was rampant. It is caused by parasites that live in fresh water such as lakes and rivers in tropical and subtropical regions worldwide. The parasites usually get into the body through the skin when bare legs are immersed in infected water.

I don't believe you would want to know all the details about all the *dudus*, especially worms, so I'll leave it there.

Leisure

We spent the first several years in Tanga without a single day's holiday. We worked seven days a week and all hours out of 24. When people come from an outlying *shamba* sometimes over a hundred miles with a sick child to seek medical help at 9pm on a Sunday how can you turn them away? Can you say "Sorry, we are shut for business"?

When Jay was a toddler we finally decided to go on Safari for a break. "Safari" simply means "journey" in Kiswahili but to most people it is a journey to a safari park to see and wonder at wild animals. Of these we had such a rich variety in East Africa.

Our first safari was to the Serengeti. It was too far to manage in a day so we decided to go halfway and stay overnight with friends in the large city of Moshi at the foothills of Mount Kilimanjaro. We hired a Range Rover and piled into it; the two of us plus our three kids, Motiben, her husband Bhikhubhai, and two friends. In East Africa there never was a problem if even 10 people turned up unannounced. The lady of the house went straight into the kitchen to prepare a meal, and as for sleeping arrangements, there was plenty of space and plenty of *godris* (Indian duvets) to spread on the floor.

Early in the morning we set off for Serengeti. It took some three hours to get there but we had more than one driver so there wasn't too much burden for any one person. All day we chased after game. We saw lions and lionesses, cheetahs, rhinos, ostriches, zebras and wildebeest in large herds, and giraffes. Elephants, however, eluded us all day. In spite of the feast of wildlife we had had, we were disappointed. It was beginning to get dark and we would soon have to be out of the Park. Dejectedly, we started to drive away when all of a sudden Bhikhubhai shouted "elephant dung!"

What excitement over elephant dung! Where there is smoke, there is fire, and where there is fresh elephant dung, there is elephant. We had our reward and saw a good sized herd, including two babies. Safaris are such fun! In East Africa with the right vehicle (a four-wheel drive, such as a Land Rover or Range Rover) one can drive cross-country on spotting a suspicious black blob until one can see an animal – or discover it is a tree stump. Professional drivers in Safari Parks are great experts and seem to have binoculars for eyes. When they spot black blobs they never fail to find an animal or identify it at a great distance.

Our next Safari was to Ngorongoro Crater: the

world's largest inactive, intact volcanic caldera. The volcano exploded and collapsed on itself two to three million years ago. it is 2000' (600m) deep and 100 square miles (260km2). In it there is almost every wild animal of East Africa except the giraffe and a couple more. The sides of this crater are very steep. There is only one road to go into the crater and another road out. One can only go in in a hired 4-wheel drive. We had to leave our car in the car park at the rim. Maasai are permitted to graze their cattle inside there but must enter and exit daily.

It was such a fantastic experience to see all the animals and at such close quarters. We even saw lions mating. When we saw our first lion at some distance, little Jay pointed and shouted excitedly "There, Tommy!"; he thought it was our neighbour's large dog. My children saw lions and other wild animals before they ever saw a horse as there are no horses in Tanzania due to Malaria mosquitoes. Their first sight of a horse was when we came to England when Jay was four years old and my girls were 10 and seven.

The Maasai are a unique tribe – tall, handsome and with distinctive customs and dress. They are semi-nomadic pastoralists and until recently subsisted only on raw meat, raw blood, milk and little else. Before bleeding a cow they tie a strap around the neck, tight enough so the veins are engorged. Then, with an unerring strike, the incision is made with a bow and arrow – an amazing thing to witness. They collect the blood in a gourd vessel one litre at a time and either drink it neat or mixed with milk. Finally, they seal the wound with a mixture of cow dung and earth. The cow does not come to any harm.

After a drink of blood and milk, Maasai can go all day without food. I have read that the Maasai are very healthy in their lifestyle with no excess fat and very low cholesterol. Livestock is a measure of wealth and is used to pay the dowry for a wedding. A woman is worth 10 cows. Women wear lots of beaded necklaces and bangles. Warriors carry a spear and a ball-ended club and paint their bodies with ochre. The Maasai traditionally believe in one god, Ngai. Sadly, outside influences are changing their way of life including their diet and I wonder if it is for the better.

More Leisure

Tanga had a Public Library. Hurrah! In this soulless, heartless, mindless and culture-less town the library was my sanity-saver. The children and I went there regularly. Surprisingly, the library was pretty well stocked. It had a children's section which kept my children busy as they were avid readers. I expect it saved their sanity too. I didn't have much spare time to spend in the library but the children spent long happy hours there. I do believe we owed our good Library to the British, so I was eternally grateful to them. I wonder in what state it must be now.

Tanga also had a swimming club. As the town did not have a beach, the club was built right on the sea edge. There were steps from which one had to go straight into deep water. All my life I have lived near water, in all the three continents I lived in. But I am sad and ashamed to say I never learnt to swim properly. I think it was my asthma that made me terrified of not being able to breathe. Not far from the club there was a rock outcrop in the sea on which a platform had been built with steps to climb up for a rest.

One day I made the effort to swim to the rock as I

felt I could cope with the short distance and I could rest there to catch my breath. I was sitting with my feet dangling over the edge when, quite without warning, a man pushed me over into the sea. The fact that I was not a good swimmer and the unexpectedness of it, besides my fear of water made me nearly drown. I struggled in panic until someone saved me. Seeing me struggle in the water the man had a good laugh. To him it was all very funny. And this was an adult man, not a young teenager. Call that irresponsible? That incident put me off swimming forever.

Tanga Library

My Balcony Scene

The famous balcony scene we all know from Romeo and Juliet was romantic. Mine was much more down to earth.

"Mama! Mama Mganga! Mama Mganga!"

I wake up, rather dopey, switch on the light and look at the clock.2.15am. What now!

"Mama! Mama Mganga!", I hear again.

Struggling to put my gown on I rush to the French window and on to the balcony. There is an Arab in white robes standing by a car in the street below the balcony.

"Mtoto yangu tayari, Mama." My daughter is ready. I understand, of course. I have known the old man Ali for quite a while and know his wives, daughters, daughters-in-law and all the grandchildren. An Arab wants a female doctor for all his female household and I am one of two female Doctors in a town of 50,000. I have looked after Salima, old man Ali's daughter, through her pregnancy and the one before and shall probably look after her the next time and in between. I expected this call.

Two minutes flat from gown to sari and half a minute to grab my case and run down the stairs to the front door. Ali politely grabs my case and opens the door of the car. In no time I speed to his house, seated next to an Arab and driven by another. I feel so safe in their company, like a goddess worshipped by them and given all the respect due to one. They expect only what a human can give. They would give their lives for my safety.

I can't stress enough that the Arabs were the best patients I ever had. I had a great rapport with them and they with me. Of course things went well and things went wrong as they do in life, but if anything went well with treatment of an Arab, the doctor was praised to the skies, given all the credit and they were so grateful. If things went wrong? Well, that was Allah's will; the doctor had done their best. You couldn't go wrong.

We arrived at Ali's house. Arabs were traders and they all had dukas. As soon as the car stopped, Ali grabbed my case and ran into the duka ahead of me. By the time I got to his door he had opened a Fanta from the duka, just as with my Arab patient Khadija from before. Luckily on this occasion my patient, Ali's daughter Salima, was on a bed and already pushing. As I entered I noticed a familiar setup: windows closed with chinks in them allowing in enough light from the street.

Under the bed was a bowl with two eggs in it. Three old women were squatted at the periphery of the room. It seemed that Arab women never screamed when giving birth. They pushed when they had to but with minimum sound. I didn't have to wait too long. Just enough time to open my case. Salima's mother had already got a basin of hot water. Baby was out without any fuss, a bouncy baby boy. Before I could separate the baby an old woman approached the bed and spat loudly on Salima's perineum (the area around the anus and vulva). I guessed it was for good luck. It certainly brought that and luckily not infection as I feared.

I cut the cord and another old lady took the baby in a towel. It didn't take long for the placenta to come out. Salima's mother bent under the bed and retrieved the bowl with the two eggs. She broke them over the placenta and all the other mess. More good luck. All the magic was really working. An old lady brought a basin of warm water and soap and towel for me to wash my hands. Baby was already cleaned up and given to mother. Salima gave me a warm, grateful smile and grabbed my hands to say "thank you" with gratitude in her eyes. What a rewarding experience that was, a healthy delivery of a healthy mother of a healthy baby. I had not done anything extraordinary but was given credit for the success of it all. Ali was ready to take me back home. But not, of course, before I had another Fanta.

The population of Lushoto was too small to

support a doctor, so once a month Dr Dapar came down the mountain to Tanga and held a clinic there. There was a massive queue of patients to see him, attracted partially, I believe, on account of him being European. Having won over the patient with his irresistible charm, he had them completely under his spell. The next move was to tackle their purse.

The mystique of Dr Dapar alone, apart from his charm, was enough to attract countless patients in Tanga who were prepared to pay his exorbitant fees. His patients were, unsurprisingly, mostly women. There was a rumour that he literally lifted his patients and put them on the examination couch. Dr Dapar came to Tanga not only with a stethoscope but also an array of magical apparatuses that could not fail to impress. His blood pressure apparatus was different from the rest of ours, so it must be better.

Whether it worked or not was another matter. He had unusual weighing scales. He had weird-looking apparatus to test blood, saliva, urine and more. Could he fail to impress? He rolled in money. He convinced his patients they were so poorly they needed a series of injections which would work wonders. Everybody who went to him was sold some 30 injections which they paid a local midwife to inject. As the problems were more often than not psychosomatic it is not surprising he had a high rate of success where the rest of us could not but fail.

Dr Dapar

Lushoto is (or at least was in those days) a quaint little town up in the Usambara Mountains. Being high up the climate was cool and pleasant. When the British were in Tanganyika, as they did in other hot colonies, they built beautiful bungalows in Lushoto. It was a most pleasant town – a feast to the eyes and away from it all. The only time I visited Lushoto was when we bought our piano from an English couple who had lived there and were returning home to England. We transported the piano all the way down the mountain and all that distance in a pick-up van with a man sitting by its side to steady it and my husband driving. We had the piano in our living room in Tanga but never had the leisure to enjoy it.

There was a Doctor in Lushoto: Dr Dapar, an Albanian with some obscure and dubious qualifications. We thought he had one of those on paper which you can obtain if you have the money. We, the doctors in Tanga, thought he was a quack. Qualifications or not, Dr Dapar had the most charming manners and excelled at the bedside variety.

Mrs G

Among the colourful mix of communities in our town there was a smattering of Goans – all Catholics. They mostly did clerical work in offices. We had one Goan doctor in town, and they all went to him for medical problems, except... one day a Mrs G called at my surgery. Short, plump and homely, her face showed great worry and she seemed close to tears. "Doctor, I am pregnant". I waited for more information. She broke into tears. "I can't have another baby, we already have 5 and can't afford any more. <u>Please</u>, <u>do</u> something." That meant she was asking me to do an abortion.

"What do you expect me to do?"

"Can't you get rid of it?"

I had heard this sort of plea before.

"But abortion is illegal, Mrs G."

"Nobody will know", she begged. I thought she was going on her knees to implore.

"Even if it was legal to do it, isn't abortion a sin in your religion?"

"It's okay, I will go and confess and everything will be alright."

"All I can do is give you some pills which may or

may not work. Have you ever considered contraception?"

"Oh, no, it's a sin and it is forbidden by the Church"

"But you could go and confess, couldn't you?"

"It wouldn't work, I would have to confess all the time"

Mrs G had no qualms about having an abortion, but she wasn't prepared to listen to any contraceptive advice. The pills didn't work, although, I was aware, she had also tried castor oil and other things purported to induce abortion. Over the years Mrs G had a few more babies, one of whom was stillborn and I think she had one spontaneous miscarriage but she never came for contraceptive advice.

Patel Girl

Mrs Miraben Patel, tall and well built, walked into the surgery one day, practically dragging a young girl who looked about 12 or 13 and obviously had serious learning difficulties. "This is my niece. She has a swelling in her stomach", said Mrs Patel. Young as she was, on examination, the 'swelling' turned out to be a 4 month pregnancy. When Miraben was told, at first she would not believe it, but when she did, her immediate response was "Can you not get rid of it? She is only a child."

Because she was only a child and subnormal, I had to get to the bottom of it. Miraben said she didn't know who could have molested her and the girl was not forthcoming with any information. We had to wheedle out the information from the girl bit by bit, and came to the conclusion that the poor child had been raped. I rather suspected that the perpetrator was a member of Miraben's family but could go no further with any investigation. There was nothing I could do so Miraben took the child home. I never saw the girl or the aunt again but later heard that she had been taken to Mombasa. I still don't know whether she managed to get an abortion or went to term, in which case I wonder what happened to the baby or the mother.

Suicide

It happened in the middle of the week. Every day, whether weekday or weekend, was terribly busy and stressful with patients at all hours of day or night, children to be attended to, and a husband who was more liability than help. Still, the middle of the week always seemed more tiring and worrying.

As usual I came home around 12.30pm to cook lunch. No question of siesta or any rest before going back to surgery. My routine was: dash to kitchen, put flour and other ingredients in the blender for *rotlis*, switch on the blender, and, while the dough was being kneaded, dash to bedroom, off with sari and on with gown, dash back to kitchen to find dough ready and get on with making *rotlis*.

On this day, as I dashed to the kitchen, I sensed something in the sitting-room and went to investigate. Ashok was lying on the sofa on his back, one arm dangling on the floor. As I neared, it was apparent that he was unconscious. His breathing was heavy and rattly. On the coffee table was an empty bottle of sleeping tablets. His eyes were closed. "Oh! my God! He has killed himself!", was my first thought.

I took his pulse and it was normal. I could not take responsibility for whatever might happen and didn't feel in a position to deal with the situation. Ringing for help would mean the whole town would know about it. I decided to ring Dr K. Out of all our GP colleagues he was the one I respected and trusted the most. I turned and was going to the phone, but something made me turn to look at Ashok again and I caught him with one eye open to see what I was doing. Hoax! From a state of terror my mood changed instantly to one of such loathing!

I went and confronted him. He was far from unconscious. He had staged it all to give me a fright. He had not taken sleeping tablets at all but used an empty bottle as false evidence.

If he had done this to gain pity or attention, it had the opposite effect. My gradual and steady dislike of him had turned to loathing and that never ever changed from then on.

Over the years he did many other things to frighten me like the time we were in France driving with the three children in the back of the car and on the motorway. Suddenly he announced that the breaks had failed. What a fright! The children were old enough to realise the seriousness and danger of the situation. What does one do if the brakes fail? Wouldn't you slow down and try to stop the car somehow? No, he just stepped on the accelerator and went at full speed on the motorway. When I started screaming he started laughing as if it had all been a great joke!

Own Home

In 1963 we decided to build our own home on a plot we had previously bought; I was very excited. The plot was in an ideal location on the corner of cross-roads. I designed the whole building: a large flat upstairs for us and 2 small ones downstairs for rental to a small family each. Our flat had rooms designed individually for us and for the children. 4 large bedrooms; a large dining/living room; large kitchen; and a verandah wrapping round the living room, facing the road. I even designed the cupboards, suitable for our needs: for his and hers, as well as those of the children's. Drawing up the kitchen was a great pleasure. It had all I dreamt of, so this made it all the more painful when our house was taken over by the government, leaving the building to wrack and ruin.

There was a spiral staircase going up to the flat terrace where our houseboy had his meals. There was a lot of space for the children to run about and I myself enjoyed going up there very early in the morning with a book, the only time of day I had to myself and which I treasured. My mother-in-law was very religious in a superstitious way. She believed in a propitious time for everything: going on a journey, giving a name to a new-born, or laying the foundation stone of a new house. For this she was very keen on doing a religious ceremony by the Hindu priest after finding out the propitious time. I, of course, don't believe in 'propitious' anything, but always showed respect for an old person's beliefs and for an old person so I went out of my way to help her.

Ba told me what was required: a little copper jug, incense, little oil lamps, and more. I went to a lot of trouble to find the required items for her. On the propitious day the Hindu priest came. He did his ceremony – to me this was like casting magic spells. Ashok was against all that but he had no respect for his mother and took no interest in it. Unsurprisingly, the magic didn't work. We had the usual hitches expected in any house building which no magic could have avoided. Overall, however, the building went fairly well and quickly.

One memorable event was that one day one of the workmen went to get a plank of wood from a pile in the yard when he heard a hissing sound and this was followed by a cobra's head reared to full height. The poor boy was petrified but managed to reverse on wobbly legs and back into the house for help. All the men armed themselves with sticks and clubs, cautiously but gingerly removed some top planks until they came upon the beast, which they clubbed to death.

As soon as one of the lower flats was ready we moved temporarily in until the top flat was ready. We lived upstairs for a few years but never got enough joy out of it. In 1970, when Ashok got the post of Director of Occupational Health in Dar es Salaam, we moved there and had to stay in rented accommodation. We rented out our flat to pay the bills. Our President, Julius Nyerere, was a socialist. The same year we moved to Dar a law came about that nobody could own property except the one they lived in. Ownership of anything more was considered *nyonyaji* (exploitation). The state took possession of our home in Tanga in spite of the fact that we had to pay rent where we were staying in Dar which I thought was very unjust. No compensation was ever given for the loss of our home.

In 2012, 40 years after we left Tanzania, my daughter Reethah went on a nostalgia visit to Tanzania. She visited the property which had by now been in the hands of the state for many years, apparently for social housing. The current occupiers were kind enough to let her go around the house and take photos and a video. When she showed them to me I was heartbroken and cried my heart out to see the state of my old home, especially my kitchen. I have never asked her to let me see the pictures again.

Our house on Goan Street (1964)

Outside the Goan Street house (1964)

Dining room (1964)

Sitting room (1964)

Jay's Arrival

In mid-1963 I was expecting my third baby. As before, I worked tirelessly at my profession and at home, cough or no cough. It was one of the many blessings I count in my life that all my three pregnancies and deliveries were no problem, and I carried on to the end. By that time my sister-in-law had left Dar es Salaam and gone to Zambia. I certainly didn't want to have my baby in Tanga, at home or in hospital. So we decided I should go to Mombasa, Kenya. Mombasa is only 120 miles from Tanga. Tanzania and Kenya were already two separate countries by then and we needed passports to go from one to the other. Despite this, moving between the two was a simple matter. Many families went on a day-trip to Mombasa purely for shopping and the city Mombasa also had several good hospitals.

Ashok had relatives in Mombasa, Nanubhai, his wife and two children. They had a comfortable home and were very welcoming He arranged for me to go to them one week before my due date. I registered with the Pandya Hospital, under the care of Dr Castelino, a Goan Consultant. As planned I flew to

Mombasa one week before I was due and settled at Nanubhai's place. I was very comfortable with them and they were very kind. By now of course I was quite used to the Gujarati way of life.

One day I was relaxing on a deckchair on their verandah when Nanubhai's mischievous son crept up behind and pulled out the catch of the chair and I went sprawling on the floor with my nine month bump and he had a great laugh. I could forgive him because he was only a little boy and luckily I came to no harm.

One evening we went for a drive. Nanubhai wanted to show me parts of Mombasa I had not seen before. "Let's stop at the Ice-cream kiosk and give the family a treat", he suggested as we drove. We got off and joined the queue for ice-cream. All of a sudden I spotted Pam, an old friend from pre-university days in Belgaum, Karnataka (in India) whom I had not seen for 14 years. She was huge – a javelin and discus thrower in her college days – with big arm muscles and round in shape. I had always been very thin and skinny and as we always went about together, we were known as Bat and Ball. We had lost contact after leaving college.

Almost simultaneously, as I recognised Pam, she did me and we both screamed "Pam!", "Mimi!" and we were at once hugging and kissing each other making up for all the years lost. The usual "what are you doing here?" and so on followed, of course. Pam was a nursing sister at the government hospital. Her huge figure with massive shoulders brought back many memories of our student days. Although greyed a bit, she still looked the likes of a javelin thrower. She was always in charge of a situation and one felt safe and protected in her presence.

In our student days Pam's father was in Mombasa but mother lived in Belgaum with the children for the sake of their education. Many a parent made such a sacrifice in those days. Mrs Da Cunha was very hospitable, and many students from East Africa who lived in the hostel and felt homesick were cordially invited to her home for a home-cooked meal and mothering. They were not exactly rolling in money but there was always food for everyone.

That was also the time when we did dissections in the biology lab – earthworms, cockroaches and all sorts. Pam gave us a continuous and inexhaustible supply of cockroaches from her kitchen. She was full of fun and always laughing and telling jokes and she represented our university at inter-collegiate sports. As it happened, Pam's family still lived in Mombasa. "Mum would love to see you, come over to dinner tomorrow" she said on parting.

I went and had a lovely evening reminiscing. Pam had a lot to tell about her experiences at the hospital, like the Arab who called one day and said he needed new testicles. Pam, with her great laugh, had told him "There are lots of things I can give you, but I am a woman, sorry I can't give you testicles". It later transpired that what he actually wanted were spectacles.

Mrs Da Cunha had cooked a gorgeous Goan meal of rice, prawn curry, stuffed mackerel and other delicacies, all traditional Goan food I had not eaten for at least eight years. I suddenly realised how much I had missed the food I had been brought up on and had had to sacrifice by marrying Ashok. I had a wonderful evening with them. I ate and ate and ate some more, like a starving child. Overate would be more accurate. Having vegetarian food at home for months on end and having grown up with meat three times a day, I craved meat and fish and always felt starved. Not surprising then that I overate at Pam's place, her mum being a very good cook of Goan food.

In the early hours of the next morning I started labour pains and was taken to hospital. Baby Jayesh arrived at 10.30am and weighing a healthy seven pounds, nine ounces (3.5kg). The delivery was no problem and I vouch I actually enjoyed all my three deliveries. But the placenta refused to come out and I had to have an anaesthetic and have it removed manually. Dr Castelino's care was faultless. All this time I was alone without my immediate family. "Where is the husband?" I heard Dr Castelino ask.

There was no sign of Ashok, not at the birth of his son and not for the whole week following. He wouldn't leave his work, not because he cared so much for his patients, but because it meant loss of income and that was more important than cuddling his own newborn son. He gave many excuses but they were obviously lame ones and I couldn't be fooled.

As baby Jay was born in Kenya he would be registered as Kenyan while the rest of the family were Tanzanian. We made an arrangement with Dr Castelino not to register the birth in Mombasa and we would smuggle him into Tanzania, registering it, instead, as a home birth in Tanga. He agreed. I cannot imagine that sort of thing possible in England but it was no problem in East Africa. On the eighth day Ashok arrived by car to take us home. We put baby Jay in a well-padded basket. It didn't look like a bassinet on the back seat. To this day I am so grateful that he behaved perfectly. At the border check Ashok and I had to get out of the car and go into the immigration office with our passports. The formalities were cursory and the Officers were too lazy to bother to check the contents of the car. Baby Jay stayed fast asleep in the basket lightly covered with a cloth. He looked an innocent and harmless part of the luggage. Phew!

So off we drove home to Tanga. Mal and Reethah

had been well looked after by Motiben during my absence. Good old Motiben, I have so much to thank her for. Baby Jay was duly registered in Tanga as a home birth and the rest is history. We were not to know it then, but when I was in the hospital in Mombasa, there was a lady two rooms away in the same hospital and under the same consultant. My baby boy was born on 11th March 1964. The lady had a baby girl on the 15th; she was named Stella.

18 years later and a Continent away the two babies, now 18 years old, met when they both registered at Birmingham Medical School. Stella's family had moved from Mombasa to Loughborough due to the ill-health of her father. Mine had moved to London due to political problems in Tanzania. Jay and Stella clicked from the start and later married after finishing their studies. Do I believe in fate?

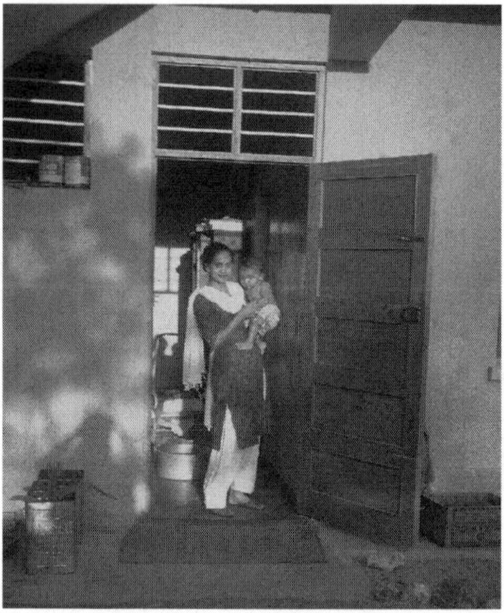

Mimi with baby Jayesh (1964)

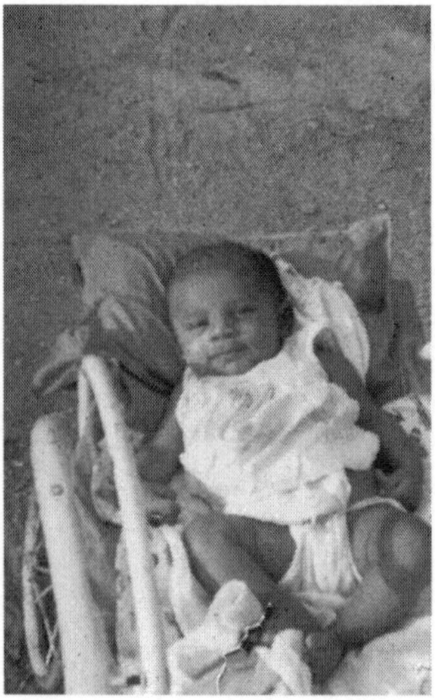

Baby Jay (1964)

Reunion with the Family

Sometime in 1963 my Papa was diagnosed with cancer of the larynx. He had an operation and could not talk. I was wracked with remorse and although I had never had a good relationship with him (in fact, truthfully I had had a bad relationship with him), I felt I should go to India to see my parents and make my peace. My brother Vicente had got engaged to Valene and the wedding was to be in November 1964 in Bombay. Papa was in and out of hospital in Bombay and when he was out my parents stayed in a hotel.

I went by ship from Mombasa to Bombay with my three children. Jay, the youngest, was eight months old. Our ship stopped at Aden. Big ships can't dock at Aden and one has to go by tender to land. The shopping area, Crater, was five miles (8km) away from the port. We shared transport with some other passengers. It was quite a feat to get into the little boat with three children, one of whom was a plump baby of eight months, and my handbag with all important documents and money. Once we arrived at Crater everyone dispersed for their shopping and I was left alone. I somehow managed to buy a mixer, a pair of binoculars (which I checked) and some other things. I left each purchase in the shop to be collected at the end.

We were all so tired and finally stopped at an Indian shop for rest. The man was very kind. He gave us drinks and the children some sweets and let us use the toilet. He also told me it was dangerous to take an unknown taxi to go back and arranged for a taxi he knew and could trust, with instructions to help me with the luggage into the boat. We got back to the ship safely. The first time we spotted another ship I took the binoculars out and lo and behold, one lens had a crack in it. The Arab shopkeeper had substituted my purchase while I was shopping around. Obviously these Arabs were very different from the ones I knew as my patients in Tanga.

In Bombay we stayed in the same hotel as my parents so we had time together and attended the wedding where I met a lot of relatives after a long time. Reethah was a flower girl and looked so cute. While in the hotel a cousin of Ashok's visited us. He sat with his feet up on the sofa and spoke in such an uncouth manner that I was utterly ashamed of my in-law relative and not for the first or last time.

After the wedding we spent some time in Goa. Visits to Goa have always caused mixed feelings for me. I love to see my old home and village but the visit brings back many sad memories of childhood mainly to do with my parents. While in Goa, TiCaru (my aunt) got me a woman from the property to help with the children. She was very good with them but got worried about the baby. "Is there anything wrong with the baby? He has such a large bottom", she whispered to TiCaru. She had no experience with terry nappies and plastic baby-pants which had just come into fashion and were very convenient but made the baby's bottom so bulky.

When I got married to Ashok, Papa had said to me "From this day on you have no father or mother, you are alone in the world". He had also said earlier "If you want to go to Hell you go alone, I don't want to come with you." So it was that I broke off all relations with my whole large family, not only my parents. My 2 brothers had secretly come to see me at the hostel but I saw nobody else except for TiLuzia and TiAlice who came together to the hostel to dissuade me from marrying Ashok. Their research into his background had not been satisfactory to put it mildly. Ashok had claimed that he was the nephew of the Chief Minister of Bombay state. My family had contacts in high places and found out that was a lie and the minister had not even heard of Ashok. Ashok's surname is very common in India, particularly in Gujarat. This was not the only lie Ashok told, both to my family, his own and even to me.

He told his parents he was marrying a Konkani Brahman girl. Theoretically one could say I was, because I came from that part of India, the Konkan Coast, and I was a Brahman, though not a Hindu as his parents naturally thought and his deceit was intentional. In January 1959 I left India with baby M less than a month old. I had no contact with my family for several years. I had a cousin called Mina, who had a heart of gold but spoilt it all by telling everyone about her own good deeds. She also enjoyed interfering in other people's lives, thus causing a lot of problems in a lot of people's lives. In my case, on this occasion, it was for the good.

She was in England at the time, in the early 1960s. She wrote to me in Tanzania "Why don't you let bygones be bygones and make up with your parents? After all you are the younger party. Your parents may not be around long. You could make the first move." At the same time she wrote to my mother "Why don't you let bygones be bygones and make up with Mimi? After all she is your daughter and I think she is sorry that she hurt you." I decided to follow her suggestion and wrote to my mother after all those years. Uncannily, Mama decided the same and wrote to me for the first time in years. Our letters crossed. We kept on corresponding. I noticed any letters I received were always obviously opened. When I asked Ashok about it he had no qualms. He said "I thought they might be writing about me". He thought it was his right to check. He did not believe in other people's privacy but would never have tolerated the same from me.

From the time I married Ashok I had gone vegetarian. Years of vegetarianism added to my unhappiness and made me long for meat or fish. I had not realised how much I longed for non-vegetarian food until one day a patient brought me a fish dish. Oh! It smelled divine. I took the dish and trembling with anticipation and mouth profusely salivating, started crossing the cemented patio to the front door.

I'm sure it was the excitement that made my hands tremble and the dish slipped from my hands and crashed to the concrete floor. I never thought one could be heart-broken over food but that is the best way I can describe what I felt. I ran into the house and got another dish. I can't even believe it but it is true I knelt on the concrete floor before the mess and picked up pieces of fish and whatever curry I could salvage, took it to the kitchen and ate it greedily. Later I couldn't believe what my life had come down to, but this incident brought home the awful realisation of the state of my marriage and my life.

Going back to Goa after all those years was a tremendously emotional experience. I could not look at my papa's photo in the hall without breaking down. My poor relationship with my father never had a chance to improve because he was in the late stages of cancer. Going back to Goa ever since brings back memories both painful and joyful. Even now it takes a lot of courage to visit. My childhood home and the beach are the most emotional of all.

Vicente and Valene's wedding.
Reethah (in front) is the flower-girl (1964)

My childhood home
Benaulim (2008)

My childhood home
Benaulim (2008)

Malini, Reethah, Mimi
on Benaulim Beach (1964)

TiCaru, Mimi; Malini, Reethah
on Benaulim Beach with fishing boat (1964)

Don't Touch My Wife

Kailash was an old classmate and friend of Ashok's from schooldays in Tanga. He came from a Punjabi family. About the time that Ashok went to study medicine in India, Kailash went to England to study pharmacology. He married an Irish woman, Margaret, and later returned to Tanga where he worked at a chemist. When we met again he and Margaret had two children and were pretty well settled. We used to meet frequently in each other's homes.

One day when they came over to dinner, the conversation turned to manners, and comparison between English and Indian behaviour. Gujarati men did not show much consideration or respect for their women and it was unheard of, even laughed at, if a man let his wife go into a room before himself. It irritated Ashok enormously when Kailash, having lived in England for several years and married a European woman, behaved like an Englishman. He opened the door of the car for his wife, held the door into a room for her and lightly touched her on the back to lead her into the room. He did that to me too following English custom. I was accustomed to this etiquette having grown up in a Portuguese culture. Ashok got very angry and told Kailash he should not do that to me and resented he should touch me at all. The conversation got more and more heated between the two men.

"What", said Kailash, "if there is an accident and Mimi is hurt and lying on the road?"

"Don't touch my wife", Ashok shouted angrily at the top of his voice. "Even if she is dying on the road!"

The evening ended sour. Unsurprisingly, we didn't meet much after that. I liked Margaret and admired the way she settled into an Indian family. Though Kailash had acquired European manners the rest of the family were quite Indian in their ways.

When I returned from my trip to India with the children, I found that in only three weeks things had changed a lot at home. Ashok, feeling lonely, had started seeing Kailash frequently. Kailash wasn't too happy where he was working, and whether Kailash coaxed Ashok or whether it was Ashok's idea, they decided to go into business together and start a new pharmacy. I discovered Ashok had taken all the money I was saving in a drawer to put into the business. And a lot more too.

Months passed. I know that every new business, whatever it may be, involves putting in money and no return to begin with. But this business guzzled more and more money and we were being sucked dry. No returns in sight.

After a few years Ashok and Kailash parted in not very amicable terms and Kailash decided to return to England with his family. We had lost a lot of money. Ashok had a knack for being 'penny wise' but also 'pound foolish', throwing good money after bad. And that was the most salient pattern in his life, one that demanded lending money when promised high interest but with no security and losing it all. This never failed to cause much heartache to us all and even into old age he continued to do this, losing everything of true value in the process.

Grand Tour

In 1967 it was over eight years since our arrival in Tanga. In all these years we had not had a single holiday apart from our short safari. At that time it was very fashionable for the people of Tanga to go on a grand tour of Europe. People went from capital to capital over several weeks. They went so they could say "We have been to … and … and …" They were not really interested in the countries they were visiting or the education or enlightenment travel would give them; what mattered was what they could boast about. They did not even find out much information about the countries they visited. That was not important. Our neighbours returned from their grand tour and came over to visit us. They had seen a lot but often had no clue where they had been or the importance of the places they visited. "Athens," she said, "everybody goes on about Athens. All we saw was a lot of broken stones one on top of another". She also said they had been to a place where there were a lot of boats, but was not sure whether it was Venice or Vienna.

Following the fashion Ashok suggested we might go on the famous grand tour. We should not be outdone by others. He made a big plan to visit most of the Middle East and Europe. He looked at a map, found out the capitals of the countries in that part of the world, made out an itinerary and organised tickets. It was going to take three months. It never occurred to me how long three months away from the children were going to be like. There was a Goan couple in Tanga who had eight children who had all grown up and left home apart from the youngest two. They missed having children around. We arranged for our three to stay with them. They could continue school as normal. They would visit their grandparents regularly and they in turn could keep an eye on the children.

I got a whole lot of aerogrammes and addressed them to the various places we were going to be, and dated them to arrive there just before us with instructions to the children to write every week and post them on the date on the aerogramme. All they had to do then was to post them. It seemed all foolproof. The children were to visit their grandparents every week and the old couple could keep an eye on them and tackle any problems. I was satisfied with the plan.

Our tour started from Nairobi from where we journeyed to Cairo, Alexandria, Amman from where we visited and bathed in the Dead Sea, Beirut where we arrived just before the June War (known to

Palestinians as The Setback and the Israelis as the Six Day War), and then on to Europe and the capitals of Yugoslavia (as it was then), Austria, Turkey and Greece, before ending up in London at the end of the first half of the tour.

We were hardly away for four weeks when it became obvious that the plan had not worked as expected. We missed the letters at every stop as post took a lot longer than we had calculated. After six weeks of being away from the children and no regular news, I could not take it much longer, and coaxed Ashok to shorten the trip. He cut it short by a couple of weeks and then to 10 weeks. The holiday became intolerable not only because of being away from the children but because of Ashok's behaviour. He was so mean all throughout that he would not fork out on food and I, who was already very thin, became awfully skinny, while he lost so much weight that his trousers would not stay in place. In Pisa we went to the bottom of the tower but he refused to spend to go to the top. In London he refused to go into a café for a cup of coffee when I said I was hungry. He stubbornly stayed on the pavement, sulking, while I went inside on my own in a huge city totally new to me. The list was endless.

After London we visited several other countries in Europe but I had no heart in the travel any more. It had stopped being an adventure almost from the beginning and instead was more like torture. The children were not happy in our absence either. Not only did they miss home but they did not get on with the host children and though the hosts were kindly my children did not perceive them as such. I had asked the children what they wanted from Europe. Reethah asked for "snow from Switzerland". It is obvious one could not take real snow so we thought we would compromise. In Austria we bought a paperweight with St Stephen's Church in a globe which showed beautiful 'snow' when shaken. Reethah, poor child, was so disappointed. Did I think I could fool a six year old? This trip which was supposed to be our much deserved holiday had turned out a total disaster from which I needed a rest but could not hope for one. Life went on just as hectic as before if not worse.

Dar es Salaam

In 1970 Ashok was offered the post of Director of Occupational Health Services, a private organisation in Dar es Salaam, Gate of Peace, capital of Tanzania. It paid very well and a beautiful bungalow by the sea came with it. We both gave up our general practices in Tanga, rented out our house and moved to Dar.

The children had to be found new schools. Mal went to the Aga Khan Secondary School, Reethah and Jay to Bunge Primary School in town. I got the post of Medical Officer with Dar City Council and we all settled down in no time at all. While in Dar, besides the clinic, I regularly attended an orphanage, the Kurasini children's home. It was a very rewarding experience and I loved visiting the children and felt loved by them and the staff alike.

Our bungalow was gorgeous. Three bedrooms with en-suite, terrazzo flooring, large living and dining rooms in an L-shaped design, large kitchen, and there was even a garage attached to the side. There was an outhouse for the houseboy with a little kitchen and washing facilities. There was a lot of land all around, unspoilt and untreated which meant much work was needed. I was over the moon with our new surroundings although we were a bit isolated. The bungalows in this newly developed area of Dar were spaced out and it was a long walk from our front door to the next.

Our day started early. Everybody out of bed by 5.30am, everybody showered, dressed and breakfasted by 6.30am, and we were off to work and school. Schools finished for the day at 1.00pm. It was much too hot to work in the afternoon. We came home to lunch always ready and always delicious, cooked by our houseboy Maulidi, as ever, taking such trouble to cook all our favourites which often involved cooking many different dishes at once.

The bungalow was near enough the sea for the children to go swimming in the sea and return home to shower. When I think back on it I could say our life in Dar was idyllic. For security all windows had iron bars as burglaries were very common. When people went to the seaside on Sunday evenings, they locked themselves in with the windows wound-up. If windows were down, a man would approach, very close to the window so others around couldn't see what was happening. He would produce a knife and demand money. The fear of the consequence of a refusal made people part with their money, watches and jewellery. Indian women wear a lot of expensive jewellery, but their fears prompted many to start wearing false jewellery.

In spite all this, life in Dar was quite wonderful. The heat was unbearable but we had air-conditioning. The shops were full of goods, food, clothes, toys, books, anything you fancied. One weekend Ashok went to see his father in Tanga and was going to stay away overnight. That night I felt very uneasy on my own with the children. My bed was king-size, so I got all three children in my bed for the night and locked the door. That saved our lives or I couldn't be telling you this story now.

I slept very restlessly. In the middle of the night I heard the doorknob turning. The state I was in, I couldn't tell whether it had really happened or I had imagined it or whether I had dreamt it. I just shouted "*Nani*! *Nani*!" (Who is it! Who is it!). It all went quiet and I convinced myself I had imagined it. In the morning I found the iron bars in the living room all twisted and wrenched. The burglars had got in and gone all over the bungalow. The only money they found was the children's pocket money and in the kitchen the fridge had been raided. The burglars ate *all* (about a dozen) eggs raw, and all the rice cold. They must have been really poor and really hungry! I remember the Police didn't come for several days.

Another method thieves used was "fishing". They used long poles through iron-barred windows and fished out clothes and bedding even in the upper floors. They were such experts that one man swore a sheet had been fished out right from over his body while he slept. It was so hot in Dar that we covered ourselves only with a light cotton sheet in bed or often with no covering at all.

Dar was situated on a beautiful bay. We lived on the Msasani Bay: palm-fringed with pure white sands, the stereotyped picture seen in glossy travel magazines of paradise on Earth.

A clinic I regularly attended was on the edge of town. It was always well attended and crowded. Many of the mothers were extremely anaemic and not many were fat. The children who attended my clinic were very malnourished and most had *kwashiorkor*, which is caused by protein and calorie deficiency. The affected child is small for age, with a large head and pale reddish hair, thin, spindly, often swollen legs and a pot-belly. They were very underweight.

The treatment of this condition is not at all difficult and if treated early the harmful effects are not permanent. All they need is *food* – food high in calories and protein. There are so many charities around the world who send food to the so-called Third World. The country received literally tons of skimmed milk-powder and high-protein powder to make porridge. We had a demonstration to the mothers on how to make porridge, we gave talks in simple words on caring for the children, nutrition, hygiene. Every week we weighed the children and gave mothers a supply of milk powder and high protein powder.

But week after week the children returned not having put on an ounce in weight and no improvement in their condition. I was always puzzled until I discovered the cause. In East African markets women sit on the pavement with their wares piled in little mounds in front of them – a few potatoes, a few tomatoes, a bunch of peanuts, chillies and that sort of thing. You can also see bits of hardware for sale. I was shocked to see boxes of milk powder and protein powder still with labels of CAFOD, UNICEF and other charities blatantly and unashamedly displayed for sale. So this is where the food went that should have been in the stomachs of their babies. No wonder there never was an improvement in their condition.

Another shocking discovery was the theft of the supplies even before the mothers got them. The supplies arrived by ship to the port. On the way from port to the warehouse some bags were pilfered. In the warehouse, several more. On the way to the clinic, the driver helped himself to a share. Finally, and the most shocking for me, from the store of the clinic the sister (nurse) took her cut. The sister happened to be the wife of a minister who earned a good salary. All these people had no qualms taking food out of the mouths of starving babes. When I went to Africa I had thought "As a doctor I can do so much to help the people!" After this experience I realised I could not do a single thing for those who do not want to be helped.

If I have ever felt disillusion in my life, this was it. My idea of charity is not giving and giving but helping people to help themselves. My favourite saying: "Give a man a fish and you feed him for a day. Teach a man to fish and you feed him for life."

Our Dar es Salaam bungalow (1972)

* * *

In 1971 Ashok went to Liverpool for three months to do a Diploma in Public Health. I was alone with the children and coping very well. But then rumours started circulating about an upcoming revolution. They got louder and stronger and we heard unsettling news on the radio. One day a plane circled above the house dropping leaflets which seemed to confirm that revolution was impending. Tanzania had so far always been peaceful but knowing the sort of thing that happened in other African countries and the dangers involved, I panicked.

After a few sleepless nights I made the momentous decision to leave with the children, take what we could with the possibility of not coming back, and go to India. We told no one but our closest friends.

We were not allowed to take any money or valuables over the value of 200 shillings which would not take us very far. I hit on an idea to take my jewellery. The children had given me for my last birthday a "safe" box in the shape of a book and the title was "Principles of Economics by John Smith". When you opened the front cover it was a secret box with a secret key. Just what I needed. I packed my jewellery in it, wrapping each item in cotton wool or a bit of muslin very tightly so it wouldn't rattle when shaken. Then I put the "book" in little Jay's school satchel in which he was carrying his colouring books, crayons, and children's storybooks. The child was quite unaware he was being a smuggler.

I was a bundle of nerves as we left but our friend Jules who drove us to the airport was cool and calm.

On arrival at Bombay Airport the Official was not pleasant to say the least. He tried to extort money and get a bribe by saying we were not allowed to take this item or that into India but he might be able to help and his forefinger and thumb did a little jig to clarify what he meant. I had a brainwave. I bandied my British Passport and said I would report any trespasses to my Consulate. I was immediately waved off with kids and luggage and out of the airport and my smuggled jewellery safe and sound as nobody paid attention to the little boy proudly carrying a satchel.

In Goa I put my jewellery in the bank for safekeeping as I had no idea about our plans. Years later, when we were settled in England, I went to Goa and wanted to bring my jewellery back. Again, the problem was, one was not allowed to take it out of India. A brainwave again! I placed the packet towards the bottom of my hand luggage. Right on top I placed a layer of Goa pork sausages, quite unmissable by their strong smell.

To my great luck the Customs Officer happened to be a Muslim. When he unzipped the bag and got the strong smell of pork, he quickly zipped it up again and couldn't wait to have me out of his sight. My jewellery certain had had very adventurous travels.

Dar es Salaam bungalow when we moved in (1970)

Dar es Salaam harbour (1970)

Jayesh, Reethah, Malini; Rex, Dinky,
Dar es Salaam bungalow (1971)

Oyster Bay (1970)

Kurasini children's home (1970)

Reethah, Jayesh and Malini
at Msasani Bay (1972)

It's Kwaheri, Africa

Every tale, whether fairy, horror or anything in between, has to come to an end. In 1972 political events in Tanzania and a fear hanging in the air everywhere made me coax Ashok to leave for the U.K. There had been talks of revolution. There had been leaflets thrown from planes. Although we had taken up Tanzanian citizenship, there wasn't much hope for a secure future for the children.

There were many primary schools but only a handful of secondary schools and a single university (one which didn't have much clout anywhere anyway).

The law was that, in education, an African Tanzanian child, with both parents black Tanzanians, had first places. Then came children with one black Tanzanian parent. Our children, although their parents were both Tanzanian but not black, had no hope of ever getting into university there. We decided that our future – both for us parents and the three children – was not in Tanzania. Fortunately, at the time, it was not difficult to come to England and a few savings made it easier, though finding accommodation, until we could buy our own house, was awful. And so, in the summer of 1972, we said goodbye to Tanzania.

For the children it was an adventure. Children are so resilient! For me it was a very anxious time. Ashok had got a post with the World Health Organisation in Nigeria whilst I got a job with the NHS. Our marriage was in tatters and I looked to the future with trepidation. My tale, like most people's, is one of love and hate, joy and sadness, worry and heartache, and adventure. People have loved me and people have hated me; my heart and head, however, remain intact even to this day as I sit here in my rocking chair.

We are off to England, to pastures new and green – and grey. A large chunk of my heart is left behind. Until we meet again, it's *kwaheri* (goodbye) beloved Africa!

Tanga (1968)

Vocabulary

Ayah: A woman servant who looks after children

Baba: Father. Also used to address an older man with respect.

Hodi: Used upon approaching or entering another's house. The reply is *karibu.*

Karibu: Welcome (literally, "I am near")

Kwaheri: Goodbye

Mama: Mother. This term is used to address any woman.

Mtoto: Child

Mze: Old man. Used in respect, not only to an old man, but even by an older man to a younger one

Mzungu: White person

Safari: Literally, "journey". Now used to mean a trip to an animal park.

Shamba: Small holding, like an allotment.

Ugali: Like polenta, made from white cornmeal. It is the staple food in Tanzania.

14397710R00122

Printed in Great Britain
by Amazon.co.uk, Ltd.,
Marston Gate.